The Transmutation Notebooks:
Poems in the Voices of Charles and Emma Darwin

by Anne Becker

Dear Alicia,
for the curse and blessing of consciousness --
for the conjunction of science + poetry -- for the
family that we are embedded in -- for the
song of The voice -- and again thanks for your
good comments that kept me pressing to finish
this [signature] 4/9/96

Forest Woods Media Productions Inc.
The Bunny and the Crocodile Press
Washington, D.C.

Copyright © 1996 by Anne Becker

Forest Woods Media Productions Inc.
The Bunny and the Crocodile Press
Washington, D.C.

No part of this book may be reproduced without
the express permission of the publisher.

Cover design by Lynn Springer
Typography by Cindy Comitz
Offset printing by Printing Press, Inc.

Library of Congress Card Number: 95-060003

International Standard Book Number: 0-938572-12-1

First Edition
Printed in the U.S.A.

For information:
The Writers' Center
4508 Walsh Avenue
Bethesda, MD 20815

ACKNOWLEDGEMENTS

My warmest thanks to the myriad readers whose criticism and encouragement kept me at this work for so many years. Heartfelt gratitude to those friends who have been with me from the beginning: Chris Llewellyn, Mary Ann Larkin, Katherine Lorr; to John Rumm whose generous aid at each stage of the project has been one of its joys; to Ethelbert Miller, his assistance always practical and sure, he steered the work outward; to those whose active support found an audience for these poems: Richard Peabody (for saying yes first), Allison Barlow, Marjorie Scilken-Friedman, Susan Preston; to those buoying me through the middle: William Claire, Jean Nordhaus, Peter Klappert—and Deborah George, there again at the end. Special thanks also to Stephen Jay Gould, who helped me get some of the biology right, and to Sandra Herbert, whose study of Darwin as a writer clarified for me his relationship with Alfred Russel Wallace. And to Merrill Leffler and Philip Appleman, ideal readers, who brought art and science to the task. Deep appreciation and love to Grace Cavalieri, her energy and enthusiasm provided light not only at the end of the tunnel but all along the way. And to John, my husband, for his invisible scaffolding, and to my son Matthew for his vocal partisanship.

Some of these poems appeared first in *Gargoyle*.

Grateful acknowledgement also to the Maryland State Arts Council for a work-in-progress grant which assisted in the completion of the manuscript.

∞ ∞ ∞ ∞ ∞ ∞ ∞

This book is made possible in part by the D.C. Commission on the Arts & Humanities and the National Endowment for the Arts. We are grateful for the support of these agencies.

For my mother and father who gave me science and art.

*Why the Thief ingredient accompanies all sweetness
Darwin does not tell us.*
                              —Emily Dickinson

CONTENTS

INTRODUCTION 11

I. JOURNAL OF THE VOYAGE OF THE *BEAGLE*

April 24, 1832 17
July 5, 1832 18
July 25, 1832 19
December 17, 1832 19
December 25, 1832 21
August 11, 1833 22
August 24, 1833 24
November 14, 1833 26
November 23, 1833 28
November 26, 1833 29
January 9, 1834 30
April 22, 1834 31
April 24, 1834 32
April 26, 1834 32
September 27, 1834 34
February 29, 1835 36
March 4, 1835 36
October 20, 1835 39
April 12, 1836 40

II. BODY OF WORK

I Even Saw a Happy Slave 45
Galapagos Archipelago: Origin of All My Views 48
The Laws of Nature 55
The Excised Pages 59
Variation 60
The Landscape of Prayer 63
My Dear Hooker 69
Sexual Selection 76
The Descent of Man: Dogs, Apes and Ants 77
Regrets and Pleasures 84
Tree of Life 89

III. EPILOGUE

Daughter's Tribute 95

PARTIAL LIST OF SOURCES 99

INTRODUCTION

Charles Darwin (1809 - 1882) was not the first to propose a theory of evolution—the idea that life forms have changed since they first appeared on earth—but was the first to suggest a plausible mechanism for such change: natural selection. Natural selection is the process by which an organism born with a difference, however slight, that gives it an advantage over others of its kind in the struggle for existence (an inevitable condition of life since organisms produce more offspring than there are resources to sustain) will be more likely to survive to reproduce, leaving offspring with this useful modification. An accumulation of small changes thus produced will, over the course of millions of years, result in the formation of new species, often radically different from their ancestors. So profound was his work that it changed not only our idea of science, but also our idea of religion.

∞ ∞ ∞ ∞ ∞ ∞ ∞

It was for metaphor that I originally went to Darwin. In my mid-thirties, after a long period of seemingly effortless change—having changed schools, changed jobs, changed friends and companions, changed location—and a short stretch of intense upheaval—marrying, unmarrying, marrying again, having a child—I felt unsettled, instead of experiencing life as wonderfully elastic it seemed slippery. Without conscious intent I had already begun seeking a concrete image to help me cope with this unremitting change, turning first to the language of geology, exploring in my poems the theory of plate tectonics which holds that the earth's surface is made up of discontinuous masses, in constant motion, driven by convection currents in the molten rock beneath the crust. Even as I realized what I was looking for the geologic metaphor quickly played out, although change was hardly done with me. Since my subject was human change over a lifetime I turned to the theory of evolution, soon coming to *The Voyage of the Beagle,* Darwin's reworkings of the journals he kept during his trip around the world from 1831 to 1836.

Immediately I was drawn in: his language was supple, rhythmic, vivid; his personality spoke clearly in his prose. I distinctly heard the voice of an extremely charming man, one who wanted people to like him. How, I wondered, could this man have undertaken such a controversial project? Turning next to biography and autobiography, I began to see how Darwin's personal life and scientific work were intimately connected. I discovered his wife, Emma, who wrote him in 1839, shortly after their marriage:

> May not the habit in scientific pursuits of believing nothing till it
> is proved, influence your mind too much in other things which
> cannot be proved in the same way, and which if true are likely to

be above our comprehension. I should say also there is a danger
in giving up revelation which does not exist on the other side,
that is the fear of ingratitude in casting off what has been done
for your benefit as well as for that of all the world and which
ought to make you more careful, perhaps even fearful lest you
should not have taken all the pains you could to judge truly. I
do not know whether this is arguing as if one side were true and
the other false, which I meant to avoid, but I think not...I do not
wish for any answer to all this—it is a satisfaction to me to write
it, and when I talk to you I cannot say exactly what I wish to say
and I know you will have patience with your own dear wife.
Don't think that it is not my affair and that it does not much
signify. Everything that concerns you concerns me and I should
be most unhappy if I thought we did not belong to each other
for ever.

Now I was hooked. It was clear to me that Emma had been absolutely necessary to Charles' work—that she and their family (they had ten children, three dying in childhood) created the foundation of his life. Not only did she provide an environment of warmth and support but she also nursed him through bouts of an undiagnosed illness from which he suffered most of his adult life. She acted as gatekeeper, cutting short interviews with visiting colleagues when he tired. She and the children also aided the work directly: she proofread, for instance, the galleys of *The Origin of Species* (1859), despite her antipathy for its premise.

But make no mistake, their relationship was not without its ambiguities, its ambivalences. Implicit in the epithet, "my dear nigger," which he chose for her to call him, is his confusion of love and power. (This choice by a man perceptive enough to point out—after a visit to a Brazilian plantation where Fitzroy, the *Beagle's* captain, naively accepted a slave's statement that yes, he was satisfied with his lot—that in the presence of his master what other reply could the slave make.) In deciding to include this epithet in one of Emma's poems I know that I am walking treacherous ground. My use of this volatile word is not meant to insult but to jolt readers who may be lulled by the Darwins' own wish to be reasoning and reasonable people, to be moderate and fair in their dealings. The irony, of course, is that he *chose* to marry, he *chose* Emma to be his wife, he *chose* this term for himself. As Muriel Rukeyser says, "What do we see—what do we not see?"

∞ ∞ ∞ ∞ ∞ ∞ ∞

What poetry causes to happen happens under the skin, below the surface at the level of the cell, or in the space between cells, in the synapses of the brain. Gaps open, gaps close, positive or negative ions stream out of a cell, or into another, first one direction, then the other. A minor adjustment in the body's chemistry—its structure—and life is now more apprehensible, more painful, more bearable, more playful, more pliable, more tasty, more joyful.

All humans use metaphor. The linking of disparate objects—unyoking a word from its usual context to bind it to further, stranger connotations—allows for much information to be transmitted in a short space, in a short time. It is perfectly suited—if not absolutely necessary—for dealing with the invisible, with what happens inside the body, with the emotions, the weight or value of things, with things that happen too slowly or too quickly to be perceived by the eye, or what has happened in the past or will happen in the future.

I went to Darwin looking for metaphor and was rewarded beyond all expectation. His own writing is studded with metaphor: "the warring of the species," "the web of kinship," "the bright face of Nature." But he didn't use metaphor simply as rhetorical gesture, to add power to his written expression, he actually thought in metaphor. The original insight that led to his theory of evolution, while based solidly on detailed observations of plant and animal life, of geologic and environmental conditions, was an act of imagination. What he saw with "the eye of the body" was transformed by "the eye of the mind." His vision: all living organisms, including humans, are related, descendants of common ancestors; that is, a family. As he expressed it in his first full articulation of the theory (which was jotted in his "Population" notebook several weeks after he proposed to Emma): "Three principles will account for all/ (1) Grandchildren. like. grandfathers/ (2) Tendency to small change...especially with physical change/ (3) Great fertility in proportion to support of parents."

For thirteen years I have been immersed in this work, alternately reading and composing the poems. I've come to understand that just as I've used the idea of evolution as metaphor so had Darwin. While his scientific pursuit furthered objective knowledge of the world, at the same time it stood for him in the place of poetry, in the place of religion, allowing him to come to terms with the losses attendant upon a lifetime of change.

∞ ∞ ∞ ∞ ∞ ∞ ∞

Exactly what have I done here? How have I taken the works of science, the documents of history, how have I taken his words and her words, and made poetry?

The title, *The Transmutation Notebooks*, comes from a series of notebooks Darwin kept in the late 1830's to collect data "on the Transmutation of Species." As I appropriated the title so too throughout the poems do I use the Darwins' own language, borrowing from his published books and working notes, their letters, journals and family papers. Yet, except for the epigraphs at the beginning of some of the poems, I do not quote verbatim. I left out unimportant words and details. Often I combined related passages from several sources from various time periods, or used images and ideas in contexts different from the ones in which they were originally embedded. After pushing and pulling the resultant conglomeration in order to heighten the rhythms I heard in the prose, I made up what was needed— what seemed called up by the words—to bridge gaps in the poems' continuities. So nothing is pure here—no pure history—no pure invention. Even the subtitle,

Poems in the Voices of Charles and Emma Darwin, does not tell the pure truth since the last poem is in the voice of Henrietta Litchfield, their oldest daughter (among their surviving children). Still, I must confess that I did take pains to get the science right, to get the history right, although there are no footnotes here, no statistics, no measurements, no data. But if my work is true it is true the way poetry is true—true to our monkey-souls—our dreams, our fears, our desires, our devotion.

Takoma Park, April, 1995

I. JOURNAL OF THE VOYAGE OF THE *BEAGLE*

If, as the poets say, life is a dream,
I am sure in a voyage these are the visions
which best serve to pass away the long night.

April 24, 1832

Soon after arriving in Rio de Janeiro, I was invited by an Englishman
to visit his estate in the Brazilian jungle. The day was powerfully hot;
nothing else moved except large, brilliant butterflies that fluttered lazily
    about.
All colours were intense, the prevailing tint dark blue, sky
and calm waters of the bay vied with each other in splendour.
Along the coast, each *venda* where we stayed the night
was nothing but a crude hut with no floor and no glass
in the windows. Our hosts were all disagreeable.
Turning inland, we soon reached the forest to fulfill at last
what had so long been my heart's ambition: to enter virgin
tropical forest, untouched by human hand, inhabited by savage
animals. Although the trees are tall, I was amazed more
by their pale and slender trunks. Here grows the lovely
Cabbage Palm, most beautiful member of its family. On a stem so
thin it can be spanned by a man's two hands, it waves its refined head
forty or fifty feet in the air. Travelling onward
we passed through tracts of pasture land punctuated by conical mounds:
ants' nests nearly twice the height of a man. We plunged
into the forest again where the trees formed a dark, luxuriant
wall around us. The road ran through the heart of the jungle
but was so overgrown we had to cut through the tangle of vines.
Woody creepers are themselves strangled by woody creepers.
Older trees have lianas like hay-coloured tresses entwined in their
    boughs.
Everywhere the eye turns, from the world of foliage above to the ground,
it delights in the extreme elegance of the fronds of the ferns,
their graceful curves, and the delicate leaves of the mimosae.
When walking through beds of mimosae, their petioles droop
producing broad tracks marked by the leaves' subtle change in hue.
In these grand scenes it is easy to specify objects of beauty
but how impossible to describe precisely the sublime feelings
of awe and devotion which arouse man's mind when struck
by the notion of such abundant life. After leaving the jungle,
we retraced our steps along the coastline, tiring
as we traversed a glaring hot plain of fine siliceous sand.

On the third day we changed our route and passed through
the gay little village of *Madre de Deôs*. We now travelled
one of Brazil's main roads but in such deplorable condition
that no vehicle (except the clumsy bullock wagon) could negotiate
its broken surface. In our whole journey we saw few bridges,
none of stone, all were built of logs, and in such disrepair
we could not cross them. Here all distances are inaccurately known.
Instead of milestones, crosses mark the places where human blood has been
    spilt.
Yesterday evening we returned finally to Rio, weary
but satisfied, having finished our pleasant little excursion.

∞ ∞ ∞

July 5, 1832

In the morning we got underway, and stood out of Rio de Janeiro's
splendid harbour. There was nothing to remark
during our passage to the mouth of the Plata until one day
a great shoal of porpoises crossed in our wake.
The whole sea heaved as hundreds leaped
in unison, their whole bodies arced in the air, seemed
suspended a moment, and then plunged back;
thus they cut the water, the sea
was furrowed like a new plowed field as far as the eye could see.
With ease, these great creatures
crossed and recrossed the bow of our ship which was running
at nine knots an hour. They would dash away
and dash back as if the *Beagle* were some giant playmate
sent to them expressly for their pleasure.
The weather was unsettled when we entered the estuary of the Plata.
Great clouds gathered up and rolled across the sky.
Thunder boomed, following occasional bursts of lightning.
One dark night, strange noises brought us out on deck
to see the ship surrounded by seals and penguins.
The officer of the watch reported these sounds to be
moans of frightened cattle on shore.
The second night, we were regaled by natural fireworks:

masthead and yard-arm-ends shone blue
with St. Elmo's light, the outline of the vane
could be traced in the night as if it had been rubbed
with phosphorous, the sea so luminous
that the penguins' tracks in the dark water
were marked with a fiery wake.

∞ ∞ ∞

July 25, 1832

I stayed ten weeks at Maldonado, in which time I procured
a nearly perfect collection of mammals, reptiles and birds.
Then I made a little excursion as far as the river Polanco,
which, in a northerly direction, is seventy miles distant.
I may mention as proof of how cheap everything is in this country
that I paid only two dollars a day for two men and a troop of twelve horses.
My companions were well armed with sabres and pistols.
On the first night out we slept at a retired little country house
and I soon found I possessed one or two things which created no end of
    astonishment.
Everywhere I stopped in that sparse district I was asked
to show my compass, and by its aid, together with a map,
to point the direction to various far places.
And each time my audience was astounded that I, a perfect stranger,
should know the road (for road and direction are synonymous
in this boundless region) to places I had never been.
If their surprise was great, mine was greater—
to find such ignorance among people who possess
large ranches and thousands of cattle.

∞ ∞ ∞

December 17, 1832

I will now describe our first arrival in Tierra del Fuego,
"Land of Fire," a land unlike anything I ever beheld.
As our boat entered the Bay of Good Success we were saluted

in a manner becoming the natives of this hostile land.
A group of Fuegians, partly concealed by the wild tangle of trees,
were perched on a rocky point overlooking the sea.
As we passed by, they sprang up, and waving their tattered cloaks,
gave a wild sonorous cry. The savages followed the ship,
and just before dark, we saw their fires and again heard
their wild shouts. The harbour is a fine piece of water,
half surrounded by low rounded mountains. Beyond this rise
steep mountain after steep mountain, separated by deep smoky valleys
which seem to lead beyond the confines of this world.
A dense gloomy forest of beech grows down to the water's edge.
That night a gale blew, and heavy squalls from the mountains
swept over us. In the morning the Captain sent a party ashore
to meet the natives. We came within hail, and one Fuegian
began to shout vehemently. When we landed, the natives looked alarmed
but continued their rapid speech and violent gestures.
The chief spokesman was old, his three companions young,
muscular, about six feet tall. Their skin was a dirty,
coppery red; their hair black, coarse and tangled.
The only garment they wore was a guanaco skin mantle turned
wool-side-out, which they throw over their shoulders,
leaving their bodies as much exposed as covered.
The old man wore a fillet of white feathers. His face
was painted with two broad bands: one, bright red, stretched
from ear to ear and over the upper lip; the second, chalk white,
ran above the first so even his eyelids were thus coloured.
The young men were ornamented with black streaks of charcoal.
The party closely resembled devils one sees in stage plays.
They were wary, like animals, until we gave them scraps
of bright cloth which they promptly tied round their necks
and became our good friends. The language of these people,
according to our notions, can scarcely be called articulate:
it is full of hoarse, guttural sounds and clicks.
But Fuegians are excellent mimics. They could repeat
perfectly each word in any sentence we uttered,
and remembered the words for a long time.
Yet we Europeans know how hard it is to distinguish
individual sounds in a foreign language.

Which of us, for instance, could follow an American Indian
through a sentence of more than three words? All savages
appear to possess to an uncommon degree this power of mimicry.
How can this faculty be explained? Is it the consequence
of the more practiced habits of perception
and keener senses of man in a savage state
as compared to the man long civilized?

∞ ∞ ∞

December 25, 1832

While going ashore at Wollaston Island we pulled alongside a canoe of six
    Fuegians.
These were the most abject creatures I have seen anywhere.
Some Fuegians dress in guanaco-skin cloaks, some in seal skin, some in the
    skin of the otter—
but these Fuegians wore nothing—even a full grown woman was quite naked,
and as it rained heavily water trickled down her body.
In another harbour, a woman suckling a tiny baby came alongside our vessel
and remained quite some time out of sheer curiosity
while the sleet fell and thawed on her bosom, drenching her child.
Why don't they burn with cold? These wretches are puny,
their faces ugly, their skins filthy and greasy,
their hair matted, their voices discordant
and their gestures violent. Viewing such people,
one can hardly suppose that they are fellow creatures
and inhabitants of the same planet. It is common conjecture
what pleasure in life the lower animals enjoy, but
how much more reasonable to ask this question about these barbaric people.
And one wonders: whence have they come?
What could have tempted, or what change compelled a tribe of men
to leave the fine northern regions, to travel down the Cordilleras
(backbone of America), to invent and build canoes that are not used
by the tribes of Chile, Brazil or Peru, and then enter
one of the most inhospitable countries within the limits of the globe?
This puzzles me fearfully—how I (or any European man)
could survive long without a garment to keep me warm,

my only tool a knife, and for nourishment no more than shellfish,
a rare bit of seal meat or putrid whale blubber,
I cannot imagine. Yet there is no reason to believe
that the Fuegians have decreased in number.
Therefore we must assume that they enjoy a sufficient share of pleasure,
of whatever kind that may be, to render life worth living.
Nature, it would seem, has fitted the Fuegians to the tempestuous climate
and scant productions of their miserable island.

∞ ∞ ∞

August 11, 1833

As the *Beagle* intended to call at Bahia Blanca,
I left the ship at the mouth of the Rio Negro
determined to travel by land as far as Buenos Ayres.
Mr Harris, a guide and five Gauchos were my companions on the journey.
The whole country we passed through deserves no better name than desert.
Everywhere the landscape wears the same aspect:
a dry gravelly soil supports no more than
tufts of dry withered grasses, and low scattered bushes
armed with thorns. After passing the first spring,
we came in sight of a famous tree which the Indians reverence
as an altar of the god Waleechu. High on a plain,
it grows as a landmark, visible from a great distance.
When the Indians come within sight of it they offer their shouts
of adoration. The tree is low-growing, thorny, with many branches,
and stands by itself without any neighbour.
Being winter it was leafless and in their place were
offerings of cigars, bread, pieces of cloth and meat,
suspended by countless threads. Poor Indians leave only thread
pulled from their ponchos; richer Indians pour spirits and *mate*
into a certain hole, or stand beside the tree and smoke,
letting the fragrant cloud drift upward into the branches,
affording Waleechu all possible gratification.
At the base of the tree, scattered all around
were the bleached bones of horses, sacrificed by the Indians
who believe this offering will keep their remaining horses tireless,
and that they themselves will prosper. About two leagues beyond this tree

we halted to make camp for the night. At that instant,
one of the lynx-eyed Gauchos spied an unfortunate cow, and after a few
 minutes' chase,
she was caught, and in no time became dinner.
Here we had the four necessities of life *en el campo*:
pasture for the horses, water (no more than a puddle),
meat and wood for the fire. This was my first night out
under the open sky, the gear of my high-backed saddle for my bed.
What glory in the free life of the Gaucho, to be able at any moment
to pull up your horse and say: "Here I will sleep tonight."
The death-like stillness of the plain, the dog
keeping watch, the fire, the gypsy-group of Gauchos,
all of us bedded down for the night—
this is a picture in my mind that cannot be forgotten.
The next afternoon we reached the encampment of General Rosas
on the banks of the Rio Colorado and there we stayed two days.
I had little to do, for the only country around us was swamp.
My sole amusement then was to observe the Indian families,
allies of General Rosas. The men were a tall fine race;
among the women some even could be called beautiful.
Their hair was coarse and straight, but bright and black,
and hung in two plaits to their waists. They had high-coloured skin
and eyes that glistened. Their legs and arms,
their feet and hands, were small and elegantly formed.
At their ankles and sometimes their waists they wore broad bracelets
of blue beads; and several of the women and men
had painted their faces red. But their real sign of pride
is having everything made of silver: knife handles, spurs,
stirrups and bridles. They are all accomplished riders,
wheeling a fiery steed under command of a delicate silver chain.
The men hunt, fight and tend the horses. One of their chief
indoor occupations is to knock two stones together
to fashion round *bolas*, and with this important weapon
the Indian catches his game, and also his horse which roams
free over the plain. Woman's duty is to load
and unload the horses, to erect tents for the night—to be,
in short, like any savage's wife, a useful slave.

∞ ∞ ∞

August 24, 1833

I wish I would hear from Henslow—it is
disheartening to labour with zeal and not even know
whether I am going the right road.
I have sent home several cargoes of specimens
and still have not heard whether they reached him safely.
This is a pretty pickle: I fear nothing I have collected
is worth a shilling. Nevertheless, I will give an account
of the more common birds I have taken from the wild plains of Patagonia,
for there are some interesting facts that I have noted.
First is the largest, the South American rhea or ostrich.
The ordinary habits, I'm certain, are already quite familiar.
They live on vegetable matter: roots and grasses.
But in Bahia Blanca, I have repeatedly seen two or three come down at low tide
to the mud-banks which are then dry, for the sake, as the Gauchos say,
of feeding on fish. Although the ostrich is shy,
wary and solitary in its habits, and so fleet in its pace, still
it is easily caught by the Indian or Gaucho armed with *bolas*.
When several horsemen appear in a semicircle it becomes confounded
and does not know which way to escape. They usually prefer
running against the wind, yet as they begin
they expand their wings and look like a vessel at full sail.
It is not generally known that these birds can swim,
but on two occasions I saw them crossing the Santa Cruz River
at a point where it is four hundred yards wide and the current rapid.

When at the Rio Negro I heard the Gauchos speak of
a very rare bird which they called *Avestruz Petise*.
They described it as smaller than the common ostrich
(which is there abundant) but with a very close resemblance.
When at Port Desire, Mr Martens shot an ostrich,
I forgot for the moment, in a most unaccountable manner,
the whole subject of the *Petise*. I thought it was a not-full-grown bird
of the common species. It was cooked and eaten before my memory returned.
Fortunately, the head, neck, legs, wings and many of the larger
feathers and most of the skin had been preserved,
and from these a near-perfect specimen was resurrected.
(Mr Gould has since done me the honour, in describing the new species,

of calling it *Struthio darwinii*, after my name.)

Another very singular bird is here quite common.
In habits and general appearance it partakes equally
of the characters of the quail and snipe, two birds which
could not be less alike. This bird is found on sterile plains
or in dry open pasture land. It frequents in pairs or small flocks
the most desolate places where scarcely any other living thing can survive.
Seen on the ground, this bird seems like the quail.
But as soon as it is seen flying, its whole appearance changes:
the long pointed wings, so different from those in the gallinaceous order,
the irregular manner of flight, the plaintive
cry it utters on rising, recall the image of the snipe.
To this genus, or rather to the family of Waders
its skeleton shows plainly it is really related.

It is also closely related to other South American birds:
I have collected two species which in every respect
are ptarmigans in their habits, and another bird
I have observed, an inhabitant of the Antarctic regions.
I know as much about birds as the man in the moon,
but I can see clearly that this small family
is one which, from its relation to other families,
although at present offering only mystery
to the naturalist wanting to classify it exactly,
may assist ultimately in revealing the grand scheme, common to past and
    present ages,
on which organized beings have been created.

Here spring is fast approaching
and everything is fresh and budding.
But how different are these scenes
from the countryside of England.
I often picture the garden at home
as Paradise, and long to appear there
as a ghost among my family, when the birds are singing
and my sisters work among the flowers, bending
and weeding, or prune unruly branches.

∞ ∞ ∞

November 14, 1833

We left Monte Video in the afternoon intending to proceed to Colonia del
    Sacramiento
situated on the north bank of the Plata, and from there follow up the
    Uruguay River.
We spent the night at the home of my guide in Canelones.
In the morning we rose early in order to ride a good distance.
Our hopes were in vain for all the rivers were flooded.
We crossed the streams of Canelones, Santa Lucia and San José
in boats, and thus lost much time. Later that day
I was amused by the skill displayed by a Gaucho
who forced his frightened horse to enter a river.
He stripped off his clothes and rode his mount into the water
until it could no longer stand; then slipping off over its rump,
he caught hold of the streaming hairs of the animal's tail.
Each time the horse turned around he splashed water in its eyes
and made it turn back. As soon as the horse's hooves
touched bottom on the other side, the man pulled himself on
and was firmly seated before the horse gained the bank.
A naked man and a naked horse is a fine sight:
I had no idea how well the two animals are suited—
and the tail such a useful appendage!
The Gauchos are well known to be perfect horsemen,
and are completely relaxed on horseback.
One day I was watching one as we galloped along and thought:
"You appear so careless in your seat, surely if the horse shies you will
    fall off."
At that instant a male ostrich sprang from its nest right under the
    horse's nose;
the young colt bounded to one side like a stag, but
as for the man, he could have been glued to the saddle.
The Gauchos consider a man a competent rider who can manage an
    untamed colt,
or who, if his horse falls, alights on his own two feet.
I recall seeing a Gaucho riding a stubborn beast which
three times in succession reared so high it fell over backwards.
With utter coolness the man calculated the exact moment—
not an instant too soon or too late—to slip off, so he was never hurt.

While on this excursion I had the chance to observe how the Gauchos
tame young horses. The process is extremely severe,
and in two or three trials the wild spirit is broken.
The horse is first caught, then thrown to the ground with a lasso.
Three legs are bound together. Sitting on the horse's neck,
the *domidor* (the subduer of horses) fixes a strong bridle
without any bit by passing a narrow thong through the eye-holes
at the end of the reins and then round the animal's tongue and jaw.
The front legs being loosened the horse rises with difficulty.
A second man holds the animal's head while the first puts on the horsecloths,
and tightens the girth. During this procedure, the horse,
in fear and surprise at being bound at the waist, throws himself
again and again to the ground, and at last refuses to rise.
The beast is breathless, white with foam and sweat.
The man now prepares to ride: he presses his weight on one stirrup,
then as he throws his leg over he pulls on the slip-knot,
unbinding the horse's front legs, and the animal's free.
(Some *domidors* pull the knot while standing over the bound animal
and thus allow the horse to rise beneath them.)
The horse, crazed with fear, gives a few violent bucks and
then takes off at a gallop. When it is quite exhausted,
the man brings it back to the corral where, reeking and hot,
the poor beast, barely alive, is released. It is not, however,
for a few weeks that the animal is ridden with an iron bit,
for it must first learn to associate the will of the rider
with the feel of the rein. Animals are so abundant in these countries
that humanity and self-interest are not closely united.
One day riding the Pampas with a respectable *estanciero*,
my horse, being tired, lagged behind. The man often shouted to me to urge
    him on.
When I replied that it was a pity for the horse was exhausted,
he cried out, "Why not? Never mind—spur him—he's mine!"
I had trouble making the man understand that it was for the horse's sake
and not his own, that I chose to spare him. He exclaimed,
with a look of great surprise, "*Ah, Don Carlos, qué cosa!*"
It was clear that such an idea had never entered his mind.

∞ ∞ ∞

November 23, 1833

During my gallop across the Pampas, I have had the opportunity to observe a
        little
the character of the inhabitants of this region.
I first met the Gauchos when we stopped for the night in Las Minas,
a pretty town, symmetrical in form, with a white-washed church at its core.
The Gauchos come in from the ranches to pass the evening in the *pulperia*,
        drinking their spirits.
In general, they are tall and handsome; they frequently wear mustaches,
and their long black hair curls down their backs.
Dressed in bright coloured garments, great spurs at their heels,
and knives stuck casually at their waists, they appear a very different race
from what might be expected from their name, Gaucho,
which signifies merely simple country man. Their countenance is proud,
their politeness excessive—they never drink without expecting you
to join them. But while making their exceedingly graceful bow,
they are quite ready—should the occasion allow—to cut your throat.

The character of the higher and more educated classes who reside
        in towns,
is, I fear, stained with many vices. Sensuality,
mockery of all religion and the grossest corruption are
all too common. Nearly every man in public office can be bribed.
But, two or three features struck me as particularly pleasing:
the polite and dignified manner pervading every rank of life,
the excellent taste of the women in their dresses, and
the equality among all classes. When speaking of these countries,
the manner in which they have been brought up by Spain, their unnatural
        parent,
should always be borne in mind. On the whole perhaps,
more credit should be given for what has been done
than blame for what is deficient. It is impossible to imagine
but that the extreme liberalism in these countries must lead ultimately to
        good results.
The very general tolerance of foreign religions, the regard paid to the means
        of education,
the freedom of the press, the facilities offered to all foreign visitors, and

      especially, I am bound to add,
to anyone professing even the humblest pretensions to science,
are all to be recollected with gratitude by those
who have travelled to the South American colonies of Spain.

We shall for the future be much amongst volcanic rocks
and I am in need of more mineralogical knowledge.
I have no idea how to use my reflecting goniometer,
and only a dim understanding of cleavage, stratification
or lines of upheaval. My books don't give much detail,
and what they do tell I can't apply to what I see.
In consequence, I draw my own conclusions, and most gloriously
ridiculous ones they are indeed. Sometimes I fancy
I shall persuade myself that there are no such things as
mountains—an original discovery to make before returning to Tierra del Fuego.

∞ ∞ ∞

November 26, 1833

Upon my return to Monte Video I was told of giant bones
found by some farm boys near a small stream entering the Rio Negro.
I rode there right away and purchased for a few pennies the skull
of a rodent the size of an elephant. When found
it was in perfect condition but the boys set it up as a target
and knocked out its teeth with stones. By most fortunate chance,
I later discovered at a place two hundred miles distant
a tooth that fitted precisely the sockets of this jaw.
At two other locations I found the remains of this immense gnawer
so I deduce that formerly it was a common animal.
I found here, too, large portions of the bony plates
of an armadillo-like creature, and part of the head
of a similar quadruped. The skull bones are so fresh
they contain seven percent animal matter. When placed in a spirit lamp
they burn with a small flame. The number of fossils
embedded in the grand estuary deposits of the Pampas must
be extraordinarily great. Besides those I found
during my short excursion I heard of many more, so that the origin of names

such as "Stream of Animals," "Hill of a Giant," is not to be wondered at.
Or the common belief in the miraculous power of rivers
to change small bones to large—or as others maintain,
the bare bones themselves grew. But I believe
that not one of these long-gone creatures perished in the marshes
and muddy beds of the present rivers, but, over the ages,
the wearing power of the water exposed the subaqueous deposits
in which they were first buried. I conclude that the whole area of the Pampas
is one wide sepulchre of these extinct animals.
When puzzling over stratification I feel inclined to cry a fig
for big oysters and bigger Megatherium—but now, while digging up fossils
I wonder how any man can tire his arms out pounding granite.

∞ ∞ ∞

January 9, 1834

At Port St. Julian, just north of the Santa Cruz River,
in some red mud capping the gravel plain, I found half the skeleton
of the *Macrauchenia patachonica*, a remarkable quadruped
fully as large as a camel. It belongs to the same division
of Pachydermata as the rhinoceros, tapir and Paleotherium.
But the structure of the neck bones shows clearly it is related
to the guanaco and to the llama. The relationship, though distant,
between the Macrauchenia and the guanaco, between the Toxodon
and the capybara, the still closer relationship
between the many extinct Edentata and the living sloths,
ant-eaters and armadillos are most interesting facts. It is impossible
to reflect on the changed state of the American continent without deepest
    astonishment.
It must have swarmed with monsters—now we find mere pygmies,
compared to the antecedent races. The geologic evidence shows
that most, if not all, of these extinct animals lived at a late period
Since that time no great change in the land has taken place.
What then exterminated so many species and whole genera? The mind hurries
    first
to some overwhelming catastrophe—but to destroy animals, large and small,
over such a vast area—and what about the fossils of Europe?—

we must shake the framework of the globe! Could it have been
a change in climate? Did man, after his arrival in South America,
decimate, as has been suggested, the unwieldy Megatherium
and other mammoth Edentates? Look to some other cause though
for the destruction of the little tucutuco at Bahia Blanca,
and of the many fossil mice and other small animals of Brazil.
No one will imagine a drought could destroy every single member
of every single species of one whole continent—and what to make of the
    extinction
of the ancient, indigenous horse whose remains I found along with the tooth
    of a Mastodon?
Did those plains fail of pasture which have since been overrun
by thousands and hundreds of thousands of the descendants
of the stock introduced by Spain? Am I to believe
that the capybara has taken the food of the Toxodon? The guanaco
that of the Macrauchenia? The existing small Edentata
that of their fecund giant prototypes? Certainly no fact
in the long history of the earth is so startling
as the wide and repeated extermination of its creatures—
now it leaves my mind reeling with questions.

∞ ∞ ∞

April 22, 1834

Two days ago, we passed the point on the Santa Cruz River
where, on the last voyage, Captain Stokes was forced to turn back.
Now it is our glorious hope to follow the river course
and by this route, reach the Andes from the east.
I long to be at work on the Cordilleras! The valley we travel
is complete terra incognita. The landscape does not change
and is absolutely uninteresting. In fact, what strikes me most
is the uniformity of the Patagonian productions. Level plains
support the same stunted plants, and in the valleys
the same thorn-bearing bushes grow. Everywhere we see the exact
same birds and insects, even the banks of the river
and the streamlets that feed it are scarcely enlivened
by a tint of brighter green. The curse of sterility

is on the land, and water flowing over a bed of stones
suffers the same curse. What Patagonia can boast of
is her stock of small rodents, perhaps the greatest in the world.
Several species of mice are characterized by large thin ears
and fine hair. These little animals swarm
in the thickets in the valleys where for months on end
the only water they taste are drops of dew,
and they all seem to be cannibals.

∞ ∞ ∞

April 24, 1834

Like navigators of old who approached an unknown landfall,
we watched for the smallest signs of change.
The gnarled wind-drifted trunk of a tree,
or a boulder of primitive rock was hailed with joy by the company
as if we had just seen the forested slopes of the Cordilleras.
But it was the top of a heavy cloudbank which did not move:
that was the true sign. At first we mistook
the clouds for the mountains themselves
instead of vapour condensed by their icy peaks.

∞ ∞ ∞

April 26, 1834

Today we met with a marked change in the geologic structure of the plains.
From the start of our journey I have closely examined the gravel
from the river bottom, and for the last two days had noticed
the presence of a few small pebbles of a very cellular basalt.
Gradually these increased in size and number. This morning,
pebbles of the same rock became suddenly abundant, and within half an hour
we saw, five or six miles distant, the angular edge of a great platform
of rock. When we arrived at the platform base we found a stream
bubbling between fallen blocks. For the next twenty-eight miles the river course
was encumbered with these masses of basalt. Basalt is only lava
that has flowed beneath the sea. But the eruptions that caused this formation

must have been extraordinarily great. At the spot where we first met
this basalt rock it was one hundred feet thick, and following the river
still higher, the surface rose imperceptibly, and the mass
became thicker and thicker. How thick it may be close to the Cordilleras
I have no means of knowing, but the platform there attains a height
of three thousand feet above the level of the sea. This convinces me
that this great chain of mountains is the source of the field of lava.
At first glimpse of the basaltic cliffs on each side of the valley,
it is obvious that the strata once were united. What power then
has removed along a whole line of country, this solid mass
of very hard rock? The river, though it has little power to move
large boulders, yet in the lapse of ages, by steady gradual erosion,
might produce just such an effect. In this case, good reasons
can be given for believing what is now a river was once an arm
of the sea. From my observations I would say that here
the continent was cut by a strait connecting the Atlantic and Pacific Oceans.
The question remains: how has the solid basalt been removed?
Formerly geologists would have brought into play the violent action
of some overwhelming debacle, but in this case, the same step-like plains,
with marine shells on their surface, which front the long line
of the Patagonian coast, sweep up on each side of the Santa Cruz valley.
No flood could have thus modelled the land. I would say rather,
by the steady action of the sea these terraces were formed,
hollowing out a valley. Although we know that tides run at eight knots an
	hour
through the narrows of the Straits of Magellan, yet I must confess
it makes me giddy to think of the number of years, century after century,
which the tides must have required to erode so vast an area.
Nevertheless, I believe that the strata undermined by the waters
of this vanished arm of the sea were broken first into huge fragments,
and then reduced to smaller blocks, then to pebbles, and finally
to almost impalpable mud which washed far into the eastern and western
oceans. There is solid pleasure in Geology! Even the joys
of the first day's partridge shooting cannot compare.
It creates the same grand ideas respecting the earth
as Astronomy does for the universe.

∞ ∞ ∞

September 27, 1834

In late July we anchored in the Bay of Valparaiso,
chief seaport of Chile. After the fierce gales that chased us
through the Straits of Magellan, the climate seemed delightful,
the atmosphere dry, the heavens so blue without a cloud
in the sky, the sun was shining brightly.
From the hills above the harbour the view of the Andes is grand,
their rugged outline clear in the transparent air, and how varied
and delicate their hues. I am living now with Richard Corfield,
an old school fellow. How pleasant to meet a straightforward
and thorough Englishman, as hospitable and kind in deeds
as a Spaniard is in professions. The country is splendid
for exercise. There are many beautiful flowers,
and plants and shrubs that possess strong and peculiar
odours—by merely brushing through them one's clothes become scented
with an odd, heady scent. What a difference climate makes
in one's feelings! How opposite the sensation when viewing black
mountains shrouded in masses of clouds, and seeing another range
through the light blue haze of a fine day. The appearance of the Andes
surprised me. The summits seem quite even, almost parallel
to the snowline. Here and there, at great distances,
a group of sharp points or a single cone reveals an
extinct volcano, or one that is still active. Thus the range resembles
a solid fortress wall surmounted at long intervals with towers
and provides a perfect barrier to the country. During my first excursion
I climbed the Bell of Quillota, highest mountain in all the Andes,
being six thousand four hundred feet high, and all Chile and the Cordilleras
were laid out like a map before me. On clear evenings
the sunsets are glorious, the valleys turn purple, then
black, and the snowy peaks glow crimson. One night as it grew dark,
we made a fire beneath an arbour of bamboo, fried our *charqui*,
sipped our *maté*, and were quite content. The air was calm and still,
the shrill noise of the mountain bizcacha and the faint cry
of a far-off goatsucker were occasionally heard. Besides these,
few birds frequent the dry barren mountains. The geology,
as might be expected, is highly interesting to me.
The shattered baked rocks traversed by innumerable dikes

of greenstone testify to the turmoil that had formerly taken place.
The whole country is composed of breccias and slates—
all modified, some completely altered, by heat. Endless varieties
of porphyry have thus been produced. To the geologist
there are manifest proofs of excessive violence, the strata of the
highest peaks are tossed about like broken pie crust. I travelled south
to Santiago, gay capital of Chile, and spent a very pleasant week.
Santiago is built on a plain, the basin of an ancient
inland sea. What an odd contrast the dead level surface makes
beside the soaring mountain peaks. From there I proceeded south
to San Fernando, and turned at right angles to the coast.
I stayed a few days at the gold mines of Mr Nixon, an American,
and while there drank some *chichi*, a sour, weak new-made
wine, and this half poisoned me. We were over a week returning
to Valparaiso, and I have been unwell ever since. But in Navedad,
on the seacoast, I was able to collect some shells from the Tertiary
formation, so that these days of illness have not been entirely
wasted. I consider myself lucky to have reached this place again,
but now know a man has a great deal more strength in him when unwell
than I once supposed. Upon arriving at Corfield's I found
a long-hoped-for letter from home, but could not help groaning
when I read Caroline's prophetic close: "Do take care of yourself,
dear Charley, you are so apt to over-exert yourself that we are all
afraid whenever we hear you are having a good time." She is as bad
as Granny who complains about my spelling. (I plead guilty,
but really, most are only accidental errors.) Now Caroline points out
the defects of my style, saying I have read too much Humboldt
and have borrowed his flowery French expressions. But what does she know
of the luxuriant growth of the Tropics—it exceeds even the language
Humboldt uses to describe it. A Persian writer alone
could do it justice, and in so doing, in England, would be called
"grandfather of liars." But I must not grumble; the version
of the journal I send home is for the public eye. I mean to show
I am more than some amateur pounder of stones, or dilettante
digger of bones. I don't intend to be a country parson, to do
a little science on the sly. I must make myself dogged and go on.

∞ ∞ ∞

February 29, 1835

Today Valdivia was shaken by the most
severe earthquake in memory.
I was on shore, lying down to rest
when the quake occurred. It came suddenly
and lasted two minutes (but time
seemed longer). There was no difficulty
standing upright but the motion
made me almost giddy: it was something like
the movement of a vessel in a little cross-ripple,
or still more similar to the sensation felt
by a skater on thin ice that bends
under the weight of the body. In the forest,
as a breeze swayed the trees, I felt
only the earth tremble. But in town,
the scene was more striking, although
the houses being made of wood did not fall down,
they shook violently, the boards creaked and rattled.
Everyone rushed outdoors in alarm,
although no one was harmed.
An earthquake destroys more than things
of substance. The earth, the very
emblem of solidity, has moved under our feet
like a crust thin and brittle over fluid;
one second of time has created in the mind
a sense of uncertainty which hours of
reflection could not have realized.

∞ ∞ ∞

March 4, 1835

We entered Concepción harbour and received news
of the terrible effects of the earthquake.
No house in port or town was left standing;
the whole coast was strewn with timber and broken furniture
like the remains of a thousand shipwrecks; whole roofs

of cottages clogged the strand. Store-houses were burst open,
and great bales of cotton, bags of *yerba*, and other merchandise
were scattered over the sand. Fragments of rock
which had been lying in deep water were cast
high on the shore. The town presented the most awful,
yet interesting, spectacle I ever saw. Indeed, I am
glad we happened to call here so soon after the quake—
now completely in ruins, it is hard to picture
that this was once a habitable place—it is wonderful
to witness such desolation produced in three minutes time.
The earthquake commenced at half-past eleven in the morning;
if it had happened at night more would have perished,
instead of less than a hundred, since it is the invariable
practice to run outdoors at the earth's first tremble
that saved them. But after viewing the total devastation
suffered by the buildings, I cannot comprehend
how most of the people escaped unharmed. Mr Rouse,
the English counsel, told us he was at breakfast
when he felt the first movement of the ground. He ran out
and had just gained the courtyard when one side of his house
came thundering down. He retained enough presence of mind
to remember that if he mounted the part already in ruins
he would be safe. He was now quite unable to stand
and had to crawl on his knees and hands, and
was reaching the summit of his pile of rubble
when the other side of his house collapsed. With eyes blinded
and mouth choked by a cloud of dust, he was safe at last.
Shock followed shock and all waited helplessly
for no one dared approach the shattered buildings
and no one knew whether his dearest friends and relations
were not dying from want of assistance. The thatched roofs
fell down into the open fires and great flames burst forth
everywhere. Hundreds knew in an instant that they had lost
all their possessions. Then a great wave was seen rolling
up the middle of the bay. At the shore it tore up cottages
and trees as it swept along with irresistible force.
Inhabitants of the port had time to run up the hills behind town,
and some sailors pulled seaward, trusting their vessels

to ride securely over the swell if they could reach it
before it crested and broke. One old woman, with a boy in tow,
jumped into an abandoned boat, but with no one to row it,
it was dashed to pieces against an anchor. The woman drowned
but the child, a lad no more than five, was picked up hours later,
alive and clinging to the wreckage. Pools of saltwater
stood amid the ruin of the houses, and children, making boats
of broken chairs and tables, appeared as happy as their parents
were miserable. In the aftermath, though, it was interesting
to note that everyone was more cheerful than one would have
supposed. It was remarked with truth that since the destruction
was universal, and suffering equal, no one was humbled
more than another. Mr Rouse, and a party he had taken
under his wing, lived the first week in a garden. In the beginning
all were merry like schoolboys on a picnic, but soon it rained
and caused much discomfort, for their only shelter was
the boughs of trees. The most remarkable effect of the earthquake
is the permanent elevation of the land—there can be no doubt
that the land here was upraised about two or three feet, while
elsewhere, it was reported, the elevation was even greater,
as much as ten feet in some places. The elevation of this province
is of particular interest for its having been the theatre
of general severe earthquakes, and from the vast amount
of marine shells scattered over the land, up to a height
of one thousand feet. It is hardly possible to doubt
that this great elevation has been brought about by successive
small uprisings, and likewise by another type of rise,
insensibly slow but constant, along some part of the coast.
At the same time as the earthquake, several volcanoes erupted
in a line running over three hundred miles northward and
three hundred miles to the south of Concepción. Hence,
I can quite clearly imagine that this land rides on top of a
mammoth lake of lava. From the intimate and complex manner
in which they are shown connected, I conclude confidently that
the forces which, slowly and by fits and starts, uplift continents,
and those which, at successive periods, pour forth smoke,
ash and molten rock from an open orifice, are the same.

∞ ∞ ∞

October 20, 1835

The survey of the Galapagos being completed, we steered toward Tahiti,
and commenced our long passage of three thousand two hundred miles.
In the course of a few days' time we sailed out of the gloomy,
clouded, coastal district, and into bright, clear weather,
running before a steady trade-wind. We passed through the Lower
or Dangerous Archipelago, and I could not have been sicker,
crossing this ocean misnamed the Pacific. I hate every ocean wave
and, oh, being sick at stomach, I find, inclines one
to think of home. Now nothing can make me happier than to imagine
that this month next year I will be very near the English coast.
Closing my eyes I fancy we are running up the chops of the Channel,
and I hear the look-out man hailing: "Lizard Lights
on the starboard side!" What joy to picture Shrewsbury in autumn;
I can almost see the leaves fall, and hear the robins singing.
My feelings are those of a schoolboy to the last degree.
In my cabin I pore over and over the last note from Granny,
where she quotes Mr Sedgwick's letter to Father: "He is doing
admirably, and has already sent home a Collection above
praise. —It was the best thing in the world for him
that he went out on a Voyage of Discovery—there was some risk
he would end up an idle fellow, but now his character is fixed.
And, if God spares his life, he will be well known among
the Naturalists of Europe." And I laugh at the last bit of news
of our brother: "Erasmus, astonishingly enough, has been engaged
as clerk to Robert Mackintosh, a Commissioner of Public Charities.
I don't expect Eras will last long, at least not if it requires any
real work." Good old Eras, he has not changed—so I cannot credit
Catty's notion that the old gentleman holds for Emma Wedgwood
a special affection, or that they will be twinned off before
I return—he is simply too lazy. And Caroline's latest message
reassures me: "It will be as if you were awakened from a dream—
you will find everything the same, except we are all
pretty considerably aged." But now, perhaps, my Father will be
convinced that he did not waste his money
when he let me spend five years at sea.

∞ ∞ ∞

April 12, 1836

For two weeks now we have been exploring the Keeling
or Cocos Islands. I am glad we have visited these islands
for such formations surely rank high among the most wonderful
objects in the world. The ring-formed reef of the lagoon island
surrounds for most of its length linear islets. On the leeward side
there is an opening through which vessels pass to the anchorage
within. On entering, the scene is curious, rather pretty,
but its beauty depends entirely on the brilliancy of colour:
the shallow, clear, still water of the lagoon, encircled by pure
white sand, is a most vivid green under the vertical sun.
This glassy green expanse, several miles wide, is divided on all sides
either by the snow-white line of breakers from the dark heaving
waters of the sea, or from the blue vault of sky by strips of land
completely covered by coconut trees. As here and there puffed
white clouds afford a pleasing contrast with the azure air, so
in the lagoon living coral form dark bands in the emerald water.

Here I will give a brief sketch of the natural history
of these islands, which from its very paucity excites a peculiar
interest. Aside from the coconut, there are only five or six kinds
of trees. The number of other plants is exceedingly limited and
consists mainly of weeds. In my collection, which, I do believe,
includes nearly a perfect Flora, I have twenty species.
As these islands are formed entirely of coral, and at one time
were mere water-washed reefs, all their terrestrial productions must have been
transported here by waves of the sea. In accordance with this theory,
the plants give the island the look of a refuge for the destitute.
The list of land animals is even poorer. Some of the islets are
inhabited by rats colonists brought by a ship from the Isle of France
which wrecked here. The only birds, although living in dry herbage,
belong to the family of Waders. Of reptiles, I saw only one lizard.
Of insects, I took pains to collect every kind. Of thirteen species
only one was a beetle. The strips of land forming these islets
have been raised only as high as the surf can toss fragments
of coral, and the wind pile up the calcareous sand. The solid flat
of coral rocks on the outer edge breaks the first violence

of the waves which otherwise in a day would sweep away these islands
and all their living matter. Here ocean and land struggle for
mastery. While terra firma has gained a footing, the denizens of the
water think their claim equally good. Everywhere are met hermit crabs
of more than one species, carrying on their backs shells stolen
from neighbouring beaches. Overhead, gannets, frigate-birds, and terns
rest in the trees, and the woods might be called a sea-rookery.
Most curious inhabitant, though, is a land crab which is quite common.
It grows to monstrous size and subsists solely on coconut meat.
The first pair of legs terminate in strong heavy pincers, and
the last pair are fitted with others, narrower and weaker.
The crab tears off the coconut husk, fibre by fibre, always from the end
with the three eye-holes. This task completed, the crab hammers with its
heavy claws until an eye-hole is opened; then, turning round its body,
with the aid of the narrow posterior pincers, it extracts the white
albuminous substance which is its food. This is, I think, the most
curious case of instinct and adaptation in structure between two
objects so apparently remote from each other in the scheme of
nature as a crab and a coconut tree.

On the second day I waded over the outer flat of dead rock
right up to the living mounds of coral, where the swell of the open
sea breaks. In the gullies and hollows there swam beautiful
coloured fish, and the forms and tints of the many zoophytes
were quite admirable. While it is excusable to grow enthusiastic
over the infinite variety of life found in the tropical sea,
I confess I think those naturalists who have described the submarine
grottoes bedecked with a thousand splendid sights, have indulged a little
in extravagant language. What interests me is the simple yet fascinating
structure and origin of these islands. From Captain Fitzroy's soundings
of the lagoon, I conclude that this coral atoll is, in fact, a lofty
mountain submerged in the sea, with sides steeper than those
of the most abrupt volcano. The saucer-shaped summit
is nearly ten miles across, and every single atom (with some minor
exceptions), from the largest fragment to the least particle of sand
in this great pile of rock, bears the stamp of an organic creation.
We feel surprise at the dimension and size of the Pyramids and other great ruins,

but how utterly petty are those when compared to
the mountains of stone, not accumulated block by block, or
brick by brick, but cell by cell by these minute
and tender animals. This is a wonder which does not first
strike the eye of the body, but, upon reflection, the eye of the mind.
It is not the beauty but the coral itself, its delicate branches
waving in the all-powerful wash of the sea, that excites my admiration.
The ocean, throwing its water over the broad reef, appears
an invincible enemy; yet we see it is opposed by a means which
seems inefficient and weak. It is not that the ocean spares the rock,
for there are broken pieces of coral scattered over the reef and
heaped upon the beach. It is impossible to view the long steady
swell of the sea without feeling a conviction that any island,
though built of the hardest rock, be it porphyry, granite or
quartz, would yield ultimately and be destroyed by this irresistible
force. But these low, insignificant coral islands stand
victorious, for another power takes part in the contest.
In the foaming water, chemical action separates the atoms of lime
carbonate, one by one, and realigns them in a symmetrical pattern.
Let hurricane and gale roar, and tear up these rocks into
hundreds of thousands of pieces, yet what will it tell against
the steady labour of myriads of tiny animal-architects at work,
hour after hour, day and night, year in and year out. Thus do we see
that the soft gelatinous body of the polyp, through agency of vital
laws, conquers the fierce, mechanical power of the sea,
which neither the arts of man nor even the inanimate
work of nature can resist.

∞ ∞ ∞

II. BODY OF WORK

I EVEN SAW A HAPPY SLAVE

It being proved necessary to marry—
When? Soon? Or late? My father says do not
wait—and if one does not marry soon one
misses so much pure happiness, but if I
marry soon think of the trouble and
expense, the loss of time: I should never
know French, or see the Continent, go
up in a balloon, poor slave, never take
a solitary trip to Wales, or travel
to America—old man, worse than a
negro, your life will not be your own.

I say: there are happy slaves. So saying
memories flood back along the channels of my mind
saying otherwise, as on the day
the *Beagle* finally set sail, departed forever
the shores of Brazil, and I thanked God I would never
again set foot in slave country. To this day still
if I hear a distant scream I imagine
that just beyond my sight a slave
is being tortured and I am helpless as a child
even to remonstrate. In slave country no one
is safe; one man owning another
corrupts all. Perhaps the women are the
worst—being surrounded all their lives by slaves
they grow accustomed to the sneer of reproach,
harsh tones of command, there is nothing
to stay their hands. They are born women
but die more like fiends. In Rio
such an old lady lived opposite me: each day
my ears were filled with the shrieks and moans
of female slaves whose fingers she crushed with screws. —No,
no one is safe—even I who would not willingly
mistreat a dog, even I unwittingly
became an instrument of fear.
During a ferry crossing when my only companion

was a negro slave, uncommonly stupid,
uncomprehending when I questioned him,
at a loss as how to pierce the fog he was
enveloped in, I spoke loudly and made
signs with my hands. In so doing, my hand
passed quite near his face and I could see
that he supposed me seized by a fit of
angry passion. With a frightened look, this
large and powerful man dropped his hands,
and with half-shut eyes prepared to accept
the imagined blow. The feelings are with me still
of surprise, disgust and shame at my part
in this scene that shows how men can be trained
to a degradation lower than that
of the most abject animal. Those who look
tenderly on the slave-owner but with a cold
heart at the slave, never seem to put
themselves in the position of the slave—what a cheerless
prospect, there is no hope for change.

But in all fairness, there are happy slaves.
These I have seen with my own eyes.
It was on a journey out from Rio collecting
specimens of parasitic plants and vampire bats.
Deep in the Brazilian jungle my party arrived
after five days' travel at the coffee plantation
of Senior Manuel Figuiero. In those remote parts
at first sight of any stranger a large bell is set
tolling and small cannon fired. With such solemn pomp
the event is announced to the woods and rocks
but to nothing else. This provides the first clue
as to the method used to make guests welcome.
Meals are pleasant torture: with such a profusion of food
that if the table did not groan the guests surely did
for each person is expected to taste every dish.
While family and company dine one man stands ready
to drive from the room sundry old hounds and hordes
of little black children who crawl in together at

every opportunity. As long as the idea of slavery
can be banished there is something fascinating in this simple
and patriarchal style of living: it is such perfect
retirement and independence from the world.
The house was like a barn, but with gilded chairs
and sofas in the sitting room; the roof was thatched,
the windows without glass. One morning I walked out
an hour before daylight to admire the silence,
which was broken at last by the morning hymn raised on high
by the whole body of the blacks; and in this manner
their daily work begins. On Saturdays and Sundays
they work for themselves, and in this fertile climate,
the labour of two days' work is sufficient, I believe,
to support a man and his family the rest of the week.
On such *fazendas* as these, I have no doubt, slaves pass
happy and contented lives.

But think back to the first night of our trip northward
from Rio de Janeiro to Cape Frio. As it grew dark
we passed under one of those massive, bare
steep hills of granite and there made camp. We lay down
on a spot notorious for having been the long-time
residence of runaway slaves. By cultivating a little ground
near the top, they contrived to eke out an existence—
but at length were recaptured by a party of soldiers.
All were seized except one old woman who escaped;
rather than being led back into slavery
she dashed herself to pieces on the rocks.
In a Roman matron this extreme action
would have been deemed "noble love of freedom."
The poor negress was called mere
"stubborn brute."

Oh, cheer up, my boy—never mind—one cannot live
the solitary life, with groggy old age, staring one
in the face—so, never mind, my boy—
keep a sharp lookout—trust to chance—there are
good wives, there is many a happy slave.

GALAPAGOS ARCHIPELAGO: ORIGIN OF ALL MY VIEWS

*If all men were dead then monkeys
make men. —Men make angels.*

It was as if in the night our ship had confounded
ocean and sky, slipped from the surface of the earth,
sailed out of this world and at dawn had anchored
on the shore of the moon—the Galapagos,
nothing could appear less inviting—but I felt
I had come home—my chest hummed with a rough thrill
at the sight of strange land: a broken field
of black basaltic lava thrown in rugged waves
like a dark frozen sea, the parched ground cracked
and fissured, covered with sunburnt brushwood
like the skeletons of stunted trees.
Closer inspection revealed that the bushes were in full leaf
and many actually flowered. Everywhere I looked
the land attested to the power of fire and heat.
Not surprising since these islands boiled up out of the sea.
The sand was burnt black. What little granite there was
was glazed and altered by heat.
There were thousands of craters, some huge cooled caldrons,
their sides littered with ash and cinders;
others were smaller where hot mud had bubbled and popped,
and was now congealed into a sandstone-like tuff,
yielding and soft, which crumbles finally
to a powdery dust. And from the summit of one large crater
we saw a small plume of smoke. It spoke plainly
in the language of fire: the days of creation
are not over, the forces that raised this land
are working still.

Galapagos—reptile Paradise—here they rule by sheer
number, not brute force for they are herbivores.
Among these hordes of monsters, the giant tortoise is
king—*galapago* means tortoise.
At our first meeting these cyclopean beasts
put me in my place. The day was glowing hot,

the air sultry and close, like being inside a stove.
My footsteps rang on the hardened lava with a strange
metallic clang. I imagined even the bushes smelt burnt
as I scrambled over the rough slopes of the cratered earth,
through the intricate thickets of acacia,
and came suddenly face to face with
two immense creatures weighing two hundred pounds each.
One merely stared at me, its beaked mouth working steadily
as it chewed a piece of cactus, and then stalked away.
The other gave a deep hiss, drew in its ugly
regal head and awaited my departure,
no audience granted. After that first encounter
I never tired observing them, for whenever I am taken
from the tame, the familiar, I am elated—
I am afraid—what I do not know
calls to me like a strange friend,
speaks to me out of the wind, fire,
fold in the rock, shell, exposed bones,
saying, "Watch what moves, what moved
and stopped, what moves so slowly
no one can see it move." My mind heated,
I thought I saw the whole earth
move—I am afraid but I am home.

The tortoise is fond of water, drinking
large quantities and wallowing in mud.
There are broad paths that branch off in every direction
leading from sea-coast to central springs.
Near the springs one sees many eager creatures
travelling onwards with out-stretched necks,
and another set returning, their thirst quenched.
When a tortoise arrives at the water
he buries his head up to his eyeballs and swallows
greedy mouthful after greedy mouthful
at a rate of ten a minute. Tortoises live also
on islands that have no fresh water other than that which falls
during a brief rainy season. It seems that
their urinary bladders act as a reservoir for water.
After a visit to the springs the bladder is distended

with fluid which decreases gradually in volume
and becomes less pure. I sampled the liquid myself
from a newly killed tortoise and found it quite limpid
and with only a slightly bitter taste. The tortoise
when purposefully moving toward any point
travels night and day and arrives at his destination
sooner than one might think. I measured the speed of one tortoise:
it walked at a rate of sixty yards a minute—
or four miles in a day—allowing a little time to eat.
They walk with an awkward lumbering gait
but they have a dignified air as if they know
theirs is a noble, ancient race; they have survived
famine and drought, high water, unbearable heat.
Like the Hindu, I thought I saw the whole earth
borne up on their backs: tortoise upon tortoise upon
tortoise—all forms of life move at their steady
deliberate pace—I am elated—I am afraid—

During the breeding season the male utters
a hoarse, bellowing roar; the female tortoise, however,
is silent, so when people hear him
they know the two are together.
The female lays her eggs in sand
if she is able, but if they mate on rocky ground
she drops them in any convenient hole. Many hatchlings
fall prey to the carrion-feeding buzzards. The old ones,
the ones that survived the hazards of childhood, or
were not killed by humans for meat, seem to die only
from accidents such as falling down a precipice.
These animals are absolutely deaf: they do not hear
a person walking behind them. It always amused me
when overtaking a tortoise to see it suddenly,
the moment I passed, hiss and fall to the ground
as if dead. I frequently jumped on their backs
and gave a few sharp raps on their shells.
Up they rose again and walked on
like a ship almost foundering in heavy seas,
and I found it difficult to keep my balance.

I admit, after spending time with these amiable giants,
I became a bit familiar and took liberties—
but after all aren't they one of the family?
Isn't it simple chance, not sure design,
that they developed in their way, I in mine?
What barrier, what gulf separates us
that cannot be spanned the way
currents move through oceans,
mountains are broken?

        From my mother I learned to love
        Nature....a boy of eight, I hardly
        remember....still....
        I see her deathbed....her work table
        ....her soft black dress....
        My father taught me about money, respect
        for the body, knowledge of its flaws.
        From my sisters I learned patience—
        they tried to improve me;
        from my brother, the importance of details,
        hard work, that you cannot go
        against Nature—I am elated—
        I am afraid—I am home.

Great black lizards bask on the rocks of the coast,
heating their bodies; and on the hills, an ugly
yellowish-brown species is common—Amblyrhynchus,
a remarkable genus, is found nowhere else on earth
but these islands. The two brother-species
have neatly divided the islands, they do not mingle.
A. cristatus lives exclusively on the sea beaches,
never roaming even ten yards inland.
It is hideous looking, its hide
the colour of lava. It is stupid
and sluggish in its movements,
its limbs and strong claws perfectly suited
for crawling over the rugged and fissured lava.
In the water it is a different animal—

its tail is flattened sideways, all four feet
are partially webbed—it swims with perfect ease
and quickness with a serpentine motion
of tail and body. One might suppose
from their aquatic habits that they eat fish.
Examination of the contents of their stomachs showed
they feed on a seaweed that grows at the bottom of the ocean.
Aquatic creatures—yet there is one strange anomaly
of behavior: when frightened they would sooner be caught
by the tail than be driven into the water.
I threw one repeatedly into a deep pool left by the ebbing tide,
and it returned directly to me, every time, trying to conceal itself
in a crevice. Perhaps this apparent stupidity
can be explained by the fact that it knows no enemy
but sharks. No wonder then that urged by a fixed,
an inborn notion that the shore alone is safe,
it takes refuge there whenever it feels itself in danger.

> That night, in my dream, I was in danger:
> hung and come back to life. A wit,
> having not run away, having faced death
> like a hero, I joked with the crowd
> that gathered to watch me.
> Then the method of execution changed
> from death by hanging to a beheading;
> but I survived, I was alive still,
> and laughing and confused,
> I showed my wound to the assembled masses;
> a scar behind became a scar in front,
> I felt no shame, I did not blush,
> laughing I revealed my imperfect flesh,
> my broken, honourable body.

    Surely dreaming is no different from breathing,
    soul nothing but a monkey—mind, body,
    everything in Nature
    the result of fixed, unchanging laws—
    I am elated—I am afraid—

The terrestrial species, *A. demarlii*,
with round tail, toes without webs, is so fertile
that it is hard to find a spot of ground bare of these ugly
lizards. Everywhere, the earth, undermined
by their shallow burrows, gives way under foot.
The look on their faces is stupid, in their movements
they are lazy and half-torpid. They crawl slowly
dragging their tails and bellies in the dirt,
often pausing a moment or two to doze, their eyes closed,
their hind legs spread on the scarred earth.
They feed on succulent cactus, on the leaves
of various trees, especially the acacia.
In the upper regions they live chiefly on the acid
and astringent berries of the guayavita, under whose branches
I have seen lizards and tortoises grazing together.
Amblyrhynchus—they are named for the shortness of their snout.
Indeed, the form of mouth is similar to the tortoise,
and one may suppose it is an adaptation to their vegetable diet.
There is no quarter of the globe where the order of reptiles
replaces in so extraordinary a manner the herbivorous mammalia.
Think of the well beaten paths of the thousands
of giant tortoises, the warrens of the terrestrial lizards,
the troops of the marine species sunning themselves on the shore,
and picture the earth millions of years ago
during the Secondary epochs when giant reptiles
swarmed on land and water: it is as if time passing elsewhere
here stood still. In the Pacific, six hundred miles
from the South American coast, a new world formed
unto itself, and a few stray colonists afloat on driftwood
rafts, crossed the deep water, negotiated difficult currents,
to find a congenial home, a grain of sand in the balance.
Since their arrival, these odd reptiles—
living fossils—have thrived in isolation. But no—
not a body frozen in one shape, turned stone—
mutable flesh, plastic, its forms multiplying—
for now each island has its own particular kind
of giant tortoise, the shapes and markings of the shell
differing slightly. And the lizard, was it one species
or two that chanced to find these islands?

Concentrate—imagine—small island—generation
follows generation—fecund lizards cover all—
slow force cracks surface—shell broken open—
lizard child more different—shape of tail and feet—
better swimmer—leaves his land-bound
brothers—new pasture under water—he satisfies
his hunger—generations follow—his
sons—his daughters—

I do begin to see that some species are forced
to change, some are replaced
and some survive—it is a quiet war
that goes on in the woods and fields
beneath the very eyes of men who are blind to it.
I begin to see how the web of kinship binds us—
these animals are mirror to my soul—not some angel
....I see her stiff hands....her soft
black dress—I have much work to do
to find the exact mechanism of change and
stasis—I am elated—
I am afraid—I am home.

THE LAWS OF NATURE

No matter how I have tried to slow this business
down, we have turned into the new year.
I begin to feel as if something real
was going to happen. It makes me dream
and ponder a great deal: what will it be like
to be married to a man? What is this fear
I feel—is it this trembling fear, or is it
something else? A rare January snow
has covered the gardens and fields.
I hardly know how to compose my thoughts;
my mind flies quickly over kettles and saucepans,
towels and sheets, such problems as which cook
to hire or how to make a drawing room
with azure walls, with livid yellow curtains
pretty—I don't much care—beauty is one thing,
comfort quite another. I try to do my share
but am content to let Fanny H. and Charley
settle which cook will suit and quibble
about the wages, the rent—
let Susan select the linen.
No, my mind does not rest on the house,
no matter how Macaw Cottage screams
for such attention. My thoughts instead
return again and again to that August evening
when a premature autumn chill made us light a fire
in the library, and Charles and I
talked alone for hours. He
was in such high spirits and I
was so happy in his company.
I knew how much I liked him then—
but was not the least sure what he felt
toward me since he is so fond of us all
and demonstrative in manner.
Oh, that night we cooked the goose—
we laughed at silly jokes—he told me tales
of Captain Fitzroy, who, he said, was

the most perverse of men. And Charley,
as he always is, was so open about his plans
and hopes for the future, for his place
among the men of science. In telling me this,
in the heat of the moment, he grasped
both my hands in his and looked
at me—it was as if a jolt—a bolt
of lightning passed through me.
I blushed to think he saw my body jerk.
The moment passed—he let go my hands,
he did not notice I could not speak.
He continued to talk of his work
at the Royal Geological Society
and his meetings with Lyell.
Outwardly I gained control; I could feel—
no—I could almost hear my heart beat:
it was like a carpenter hammering nails
when hammer blows echo in an empty room.
I don't know why when again I went to speak
I spoke of God, and Charles confessed
his doubts to me: during his voyage, he said,
less and less did he see the earth as product
of God's great plan. More and more, he said,
he sensed the force of the laws of nature.
But what, I wonder, are
the laws of nature if not the workings
of God's hand?—*I am the vine;*
My Father is the husbandman.—
And then again he clasped my hand,
he did not want his doubts to distress me.
I did not pull away but I did not
look at him—I'm glad Charley is a busy man—
After that night I dared hope if he saw
more of me he would really like me too,
but I was unprepared for that November Sunday
when next we met and he asked me to marry him.
All his letters between August and November
did not reveal to me how his feelings had grown.—

I am the vine—Now each time he writes me, chafing
at the time I need to prepare myself for our new life,
he declares, every time he thinks of the hours we spent
alone together his heart is sick
to make me his wife.—*I am the vine.*
He that abides in Me and I in him,
the same brings forth much fruit:
but without Me you can do nothing—
Unlike myself now I grow dreamy,
now I must feel the same sickness
for it is like the weakness that comes
over one, the knees buckle and one faints.
When Charley writes, "Like a child
that has something it loves beyond measure,
I long to dwell on the words, *my own*, my dear
Emma," —*I am the vine,*
you are the branches—
he says don't show anyone his letters.
What a silly fear, for to whom could I explain
how I feel—*I am the vine*—what words have I
to describe this mixture of weakness and power,
this kind of joy that is a bodily ache,
this fear that smothers me, that leaves me
without breath or speech? Could I tell
the half of this to Elizabeth, to Charlotte?
Could I tell my sweetest Mama? Even if her mind
was whole still? Even if she was the same dear Mama
I confided all my childish fears to?
I half see her face, as it was then, as it seems
still, calm and kind, her eyes
looking into mine as if she read there
what I really feared, what I wanted.
Now what will I write Charley?
Something to amuse him. I know—
I'll tell him how our news travelled the family
grapevine, from aunt to uncle, from cousin to cousin,
until it reached Cousin John at Oxford, changed slightly
so he understood the happy couple to wed

was Emma Wedgwood and Dr Darwin.
How tactfully he expressed his doubts
about this union: "There must be some
disparity of age," he wrote Aunt Fanny.
If I know my Charley, he too
must feel this fear as the day we join our lives
together draws near—he says his head
aches so lately. This comforts me:
to think that no matter how great the difference
in our manners, in our tempers, in our very
natures, the void is not so awfully great—
although I could not confide my fear to him.

THE EXCISED PAGES

> *My God, it is intolerable to think of*
> *one's whole life, like a neuter bee,*
> *working, working & nothing after all.—*
> *No, no, it won't do.*

Last night I dreamed of my own, my dear
Emma, and now I know there is no limit
to man's desire, it comes not with a scent,
a stance, a time of year, but oh it does
with a willing woman, her long and heavy hair
unloosed, the wind moist and hot in my lungs,
a stormy tropical sea, a gale seen from shore,
waving trees, the wild flight of birds, dark shadows
and bright lights, the rushing of torrents, the mountainous
waves, we are panting like dogs, side and flanks
heave, a hard run in summer heat, we shiver
like leaves, from fear, from heat—what passes
in a man's mind when he says he loves
someone, the clear features of the one he loves?
—the thighs, the twin white breasts like sails
filled, the blue hot sky—or the primeval
forest teeming with life, a wild devotion
to growth, the tangled vines, the smooth round
arms—or is it blind? a shudder of pleasure in
white heat, heart beats wildly against the ribs, nostrils
quiver—I think of E. and blood rushes everywhere,
all at once, face, chest, my penis
burns and rises, oh noble beast, I am red,
a baboon, I am she, she is me, I long to kiss, to
bite the flesh I love, to touch, touch,
oh, I am a brute for work,
oh, Mammy, I am a slave of love.

VARIATION

Eight years I laboured at my task, at the dissection
and description of my Cirripedes; although in that time
two entire years were lost to bouts of illness
when my stomach was so racked with pain I could not
work. Whole days went by when I could do no more
than lie on the sofa while my dear Emma read to me,
and if I slept she kept on reading aloud, believing
the sound of her voice helped me sleep. Or I went

for the water cure, days spent wrapped in cold,
wet sheets and this enabled me to work again—although
how it helped I do not know. In those eight years
how I came to hate them, these creatures with their
shells, some stalked and some attached directly to a rock,
or a whale, or to the bottom of boats, whatever is awash
in water. And how, at times, I felt such joy and wonder
as when on my *Beagle* voyage I discovered in Chile

a new form which differed so from all the others
that it required a new sub-order for its sole
reception. Now when I was young, my father and
my masters considered me an ordinary boy; I confess
I did not care much for the classics nor my assigned
subjects in school, but in a fit of unjust anger,
my father, usually the kindest man, declared that I
cared for nothing but dogs and shooting and rat-

catching; I would disgrace my family, he
predicted. While I have no great quickness of wit
and apprehension, and no more inventiveness or
common sense than any successful doctor or lawyer,
and my memory though extensive is hazy,
and my power to follow a long and purely abstract
train of thought has its limits, on the favourable
side of the balance, I think I can truly say

I am superior in noticing things that easily escape
attention, my industry could not have been greater
in the observation and collection of facts. Since
my earliest youth I have had the strongest desire
to understand what I observed: to bring order
to the chaos of fact. This is how I came to
undertake this mammoth task—to understand this one,
my *Balanus arthrobalanus*, I had to study all.

So for those eight years it was as if
a slow current flowed through Down
House depositing barnacles that day after day,
under scalpel and microscope, gave up their secrets.
In those eight years my children accepted barnacles
as a common household item, if not a necessity,
their dissection as a usual occupation.
My description of a larval cirripede

with six pairs of beautifully constructed
natatory legs, a pair of magnificent compound
eyes, and extremely complex antennae caused them
much amusement, an advertisement for barnacles,
they quizzed me. During those eight years I
discovered the cementing apparatus—although
I blundered dreadfully on the cement glands—
I came to know barnacles as a parent knows

his children, how each is alike, how
each is different, as if one had got their mother's
hands, another the shape of their father's head. What
diversity there is, even in these simpler creatures,
and for me how pleasant is variation. I discovered too,
perhaps the most remarkable barnacle of all: among these
animals most are hermaphrodite, carrying out the duties
of both sexes. But this strange one, I suspect, is the most

negative of creatures: males who have no mouth, no
stomach or thorax, no limbs or abdomen, they consist

wholly of the male organs in an envelope. What
started as a little zoology grew and grew
into a great beast for I could not do less—
despite illness and the interruption of children
I hung on to my study like grim death—how
else had I the right to examine this question:

what accounts for variation,
unless I myself described many
species. No, I could not abandon my sea
creatures in midstream, I had to swim doggedly
through them all. What I have learned now fills
four volumes, but in truth never has a mountain
of labour brought forth such a mouse—
I do not know if it was worth it.

That there are laws of inheritance I have no doubt,
but what they are I have yet to find out.

THE LANDSCAPE OF PRAYER

The children, thank God, are all well at present;
we are so awfully used to colds and fevers
among the chickens—then I must divide my time
between them and Papa, who is apt to be unwell
any day. Even little Charley, our poor baby,
born to us late with something lacking in his
brain, his eyes rarely focus on our faces,
even he has performed his first smiles lately,
but what it is that delights him I cannot tell.
I will not hope too much for Papa, with an invalid
I find unusual health goes before a fall.
And, thank God, even I have slept well these last
few days with no regrets to keep me awake and turning.
Tomorrow I must pay a call on Mrs B., who has
come home no better. I wish that she
and her poor mother could be smothered, and James D.
in the same batch, as I hear he is going
blind and his business is failing. I am satisfied
that Miss P. has been confined to an Asylum
that will care for her as best can be, but
whether there is any cure for her insanity
I do not know. How I could have failed
to notice her peculiarities staggers me, although
she never harmed the children. I must question
the next one more closely. Not until
she began teaching the girls a language
spoken in no country known to me, and wandered
the woods and fields of Downe at night as if she
searched for something lost in sleep did I
recognize the derangement of her mind. I cannot
hope to find another governess like Miss Thorley
who loved the chickens like her own and nursed
Annie in her last illness when I could not
be with her as my ninth confinement was due
within the month. How bitter it is
to have a treasure lost—to not see her,

not to have offered one last comfort, not to have
laid my hand on her forehead, felt her hand
on my arm—she, who never concealed a thought,
was so affectionate and forgiving.
The gap a child leaves
is not filled by another—what I have left
is a half-finished piece of needlework,
a few lessons copied out in her childish hand,
and two pocket-books. But it is memory
that fleshes out dead matter and memory
is strong in me. I suppose I should care more
about the children's lessons, but other than
a knowledge of spelling and good handwriting
I wish only for them to be right in the heart,
later they will learn for themselves
what they need. Mornings
I must try to keep the chickens out of
Charles' study; he is hard at work
on his species book and it costs him
much fretting as he says it must be perfect
as ever he can make it. But
they constantly run in and out with demands for
string and paper. "Oh, we know Papa's mornings are
sacred to work, but we work too, and our need is
urgent," says Lenny. I will coax them with a
shilling to come to me first with their desperate
business. How grateful I am to the pigeons
for they distract Charles from his pains
and worries—and I almost wish again
for the incessant barnacles for when
my dear Nigger had a load of them to study
and dissect, the gas and acid in his stomach
seemed to dissipate and days would pass without that
terrible retching and the languor, dizziness, the sinking
feelings that remain after the pain has lifted. But it is
a great happiness to me that when Charles is most unwell
he continues as sociable as ever. He is not like the rest
of the Darwins, who will not say how they really are.

But he always tells me how he feels and never wants
to be alone, he continues as affectionate as ever
so that I feel I am a comfort to him. Today all day
a strong wind blew from the southwest just
as I like it so that by evening one could taste
salt on the drawing room windows although we are
forty miles from the sea. Pale blue
violets, primroses and wood anemones have all just
opened their eyes. Soon traveller's joy and byronies
will bloom in the hedges. The first leaves, tender reds
and greens, are uncurling their fists; elm buds
glow purplish. It is early spring,
my favourite time of year at Down
now that I am used to the chalklands
of the south. Early mornings I drift in
and out of sleep like an unmanned boat
floating into shore. Our days go
like clock-work, each like the other,
the regularity is such an element of happiness
to me. Breakfast is always at eight,
followed first by work for one hour and a half,
then intervals of exercise, rest and reading.
The books we pick in the mornings
are the "serious" books of the day: travels,
memoirs and history (if not too stiff).
The walk is a turn round the Sand-Walk,
Charles' "thinking path," down to the sand pit
and back, past my wild garden where I applied my own
natural selection. I pulled Dog's Mercury and Jack-
in-the-Hedges to give bluebells and wild ivy space
to grow. Untidy as I am in the house, I like to
clear out brush, carve and cut among the shrubs.
We lunch all together at one, Charles and the children
and me. This is when I miss my older sons—we dared not
keep them from school and risk they be unprepared
for the ordeal of life to come—I try not to worry
too much, for boys (and schools) are better these days
than when I was young. Our meals are simple but

never quiet—how could they be with five children
at the table. Luncheon over, Charles reads the *Times*
and answers his mail, which leaves me free to visit
the poor and ailing. I must confess I do not miss
my daily stop at Petleys since Aunt Sarah died,
for aside from our charities we had nothing
in common and our talk was full of awkward
silence although I think she did not mind since
social intercourse was neither a duty nor
a desire. Her life was all in her books
and her philanthropy, and while she moved
from Staffordshire to Downe to live near me,
her favourite niece, it was enough, I think,
to see me every day—what we said was of no consequence.
While she declared Willy a charming baby before
he learned to speak, her stern demeanor
frightened the chickens and I never required
that they accompany me. I picture her so precisely,
tall and thin in her scanty lilac muslin,
an old fashioned leghorn bonnet, her shoulders
layered with shawls. She always wore gloves
whether indoors or out. White gloves for reading
she changed to black for dirty tasks, such as
putting coal on the fire or when
she had to shake hands with a child. How vividly
I see her face, eyes bright with horror, lips pulled
straight, the day Willy overhead us talk about
a poor dog crushed by a railroad train, and he expressed
such desire to have seen it. I know she thought
he took delight in the dog's gruesome death. Late
afternoons I read again to Charles who lies on the sofa.
This time we choose a novel with a pretty girl that Charles
can fall in love with, and a happy ending. Miss Austen
suits us well then: I like her wit and her moderation
of feeling. Charles works again before supper, one hour
and a half if he is rested, and I busy myself with the
children or hear the servants' complaints and their problems.
Supper's at seven and two games of backgammon

religiously follow—Charles wins most games but I win
most gammons. Evenings when he feels strong enough
he reads to us which delights the children, they are
so awfully used to the sound of my voice reading.
Charles is in bed by half past ten, although sleep
eludes him for several more hours. Late at night
is my time to be perfectly quiet, when the house
sleeps around me. I choose a book that suits
my taste only, essays perhaps, or philosophy,
or political history. Or I do my needlework,
knit caps and vests for the children,
a bit of delicate embroidery, which soothes me
more than reading. When I mount the stairs
to join my dear Nigger in bed, he always greets me
with a tender and gracious word of welcome
no matter how poorly he feels. And this is why
I love him: everything I do for him is answered
with such gratitude however small the service,
a sip of tea offered when his lips are parched
from constant retching, the placement of a pillow
corrected. He has even said, "It is almost
worthwhile to be sick since I am nursed by you."
Soon I must write to Willy at Rugby; I will copy out
the old Wedgwood rhyme: "Write, write, write a letter!
Good advice will make us better, /Sisters, Brothers,
Father, Mother, /Let us all advise each other." That
will amuse him. Then I must remind him when it is his turn
at morning chapel to read from the Bible
he might study the chapter before hand so that he knows
what it means. In this way he will do his own soul good
and set George an example—for what good is
our devotion if it makes no sense? Perhaps this summer
Charles will agree to go to the Aunts at Tenby,
a rest by the sea would set us all to rights. The thought
of travelling knocks him up but the change of air
and the trip itself restore him. Charles is so prone
to overwork, and the species question—how they are created
and how they change—causes much anxiety. He has made me

trustee. I wish he could smoke a pipe or
ruminate like a cow; he worries how his friends will receive
this enquiry, they will think him presumptuous, he fears,
like confessing murder is how he feels it.
The facts are interesting but the theory
I dislike as it puts God further off,
for there are some things
that his science doesn't answer, some truths
cannot be proved through reason or the most ingenious
experimentation. His dread, I think, slows
the writing. What worries him worries me,
and I mind his suffering almost as much as I mind
my own. The only relief I find
is to take as from God's hand, and try and believe
that all suffering and illness is meant to exalt us.
So I try to look forward with hope
to a time to come. And when I see Charles' patience,
his self command, and above all,
his devotion, I long to see these feelings directed
upward as well as to the one who values them most
on earth. Is it
presumptuous of me to think this?
I find it difficult enough in my own case.
So many years have passed
since I promised my dear Charley
not to bother him with worries of this nature—
but truly nothing is forbidden between us.
I often think of the words: "Thou shalt
keep him in perfect peace whose mind
is stayed on thee." It is
feeling, not reasoning
that drives me to prayer.

MY DEAR HOOKER

You ask how I am—I work a little every day
with groans and sighs, chipping away
at the mountain of facts I have compiled.
Oh, I am dull as a fig. Before that
I had five pretty good days and before that
I spent fully a third of my time in bed.
You ask how I am—the work is
turning out badly and I am sick at heart.
All Nature is perverse and will not do
as I want. Like Croesus
I am overwhelmed by my riches of facts
and fear my long-planned-for book will prove
to be nothing but an empty puffball.
My cousin Fox does me an injustice: he claims
the desire for fame drives me to this work.
While I do confess to a wish to
stagger the great guns slightly,
if I know myself at all, I work
from a sort of instinct to make out the truth.
Ever since my voyage on the *Beagle*
the course of my life has been set: to unravel
the mysteries of all those strange and
funny little facts after my own heart
that bear on the place of each species
in the economy of Nature. I never cease
to marvel that except for two small circumstances
my life would have been entirely different.
I was a dutiful son and since (although I tried)
I could not follow my father's profession
as physician, having no stomach, as you well know,
for the practice of surgery, I agreed to
his second choice: for me to join the clergy.
A voyage round the world he felt could serve
no purpose but to delay the start
of my vocation. Not to go against his wishes
I declined to apply for the position

with Captain Fitzroy. Had not Emma's father,
my own Uncle Jos, insisted on driving me
the thirty miles from Maer to Shrewsbury
to convince my father that one reasonable man
held the voyage to be a positive good for me,
and had not Fitzroy put aside his own conviction
that the shape of my forehead and nose
doomed our relationship, I would now be
explaining God to my parishioners
instead of attending to my pigeons
and my grasses. —Is it not astonishing
how such small and obscure forces
decide a creature's fate?

Since that voyage I have had one task,
when novelty allowed free range to my imagination
giving rise to speculation on the meaning
of it all. In Patagonia, where I saw
plains of gravel and dust worn everywhere
into deep gullies—there is not a tree
nor scarcely an animal or bird, all is
stillness and desolation—what strange pleasure
was excited in me and I asked
for how many ages had these plains thus lasted
and for how many more were they doomed
to continue? And the mountains of southern Chile,
those solid masses of granite, destitute
of vegetation, capped with mica-slate,
eroded in sharp stone fingers, which seemed
coeval with the beginning of the world—how long
had they lasted? With the fossil bones I uncovered
I built castles in the air, so in my mind's eye
I beheld a South American continent aswarm
with monsters, giant versions of the same
species that now inhabit these places.
From that moment I suspected that the wondrous
relation between the dead and the living
would shed light on the appearance of

organic beings on earth. And when I saw
how every part of the world is
habitable—even those regions
deemed most inhospitable and barren
all support some kind of life,
whether lakes of brine, hot mineral springs,
the wide expanse and depths of the oceans,
or even the surface of perpetual snow—
I began to understand how all
life is suited to its home.
And I saw too that the crust of the earth,
considered since earliest childhood the emblem
of that which is solid and endures, is constantly in
motion and prone to change, not usually
in a sudden awesome fashion as catastrophists claim,
but in a slow gradual manner over unimaginable years
have the mountains been uplifted, the shorelines
moved, although I cannot accept the theory
you hold dear of a former connection
of the South American continent, New Zealand
and all the Antarctic Islands.

My dear Hooker, how candidly and meekly
you took my Jeremiad on your severity to
second-class men. After my last letter,
an ugly little voice was raised asking
how much of my defense of the poor in fact
and spirit was due to your not seldom smashing
my favourite notions. While at times
I despise myself as a poor compiler
as heartily as you could do, I do not
despise my whole work for I think I have
laid the foundation for a discussion
of the origin of species. Although sometimes
I do despair that the abstract I now write
must be imperfect as I can only give
the general conclusions of twenty years' work—
with a few facts for illustration.

No one can feel more sensible than I
of the need hereafter of publishing all the facts,
with references, for I am all too aware
that there is scarcely a single point I raise
that could not lead to conclusions
directly opposite the ones I made.
How humiliating! How disgusting!

Wallace asks whether I shall discuss man—
it is a subject so surrounded by prejudice
I think I will avoid the whole topic entirely.
But how often am I made wroth by that arrogance
which caused our forefathers to claim for man
and God a special relation and to believe
we are a product of a separate act of creation.
Our self-admiration—what trash! —blinds us
to the fact that man and all vertebrate animals
are constructed on the same general model.
But animals we have made our slaves,
we do not like to consider our equals—
do not slave holders wish to make the black man
have other mind? —But animals, our fellow brethren
in pain and suffering, they know fear and affection,
respect and sorrow in death—why should we think ourselves
better? No, Hooker, it is obvious, we are all netted
together. Our ancestors came from the sea, breathed
water, had a swim bladder, and a great swimming
tail, their skulls were imperfectly formed, and each
had the organs of both sexes. Here
is a pleasant genealogy for men! Man
is not God, nor a child of God—our end
will come under the present form; like any animal
we act and are acted upon by organic and
inorganic agents of the earth. Men
like Mastodons will fade away, we will be no more
than old bones and whatever ruins of our lives
that persist. Oh, Hooker, when we are in our graves
the day will come when all the laws of change

are thought the most important part of the
science we love.

Dear friend, of all the aid I have been given
in this immense study, it is to you I owe
the biggest obligation. Since the beginning
when you made out for me the botany
of the Galapagos Archipelago and confirmed that
there was something strange in the fact that life
on those rocky islands bears the stamp
of the American continent although the climate
and geology are nothing like. And yet
each island has its own particular species of mock-thrush
and tortoise, of finch and of numerous plants,
varying as they do from island to island,
all within sight of each other, all living
at the same elevation, surviving in the same climate,
I wondered what caused the likenesses, what
made them different. You have followed me patiently
step by step. Botanical ignoramus that I am
you have answered my hundreds—no—my thousands
of questions. But it is the sad truth, Hooker,
that accustomed as I am, from being quizzed
by my non-naturalist relations, to expect contempt
and contradiction, I have all too often forgotten
that you are the one soul living
who has been constant. How I treasure
your deep and open mind before which
I could uncover my wildest speculation.
And not least of the help you have given me
has been your visits to Down when we talked
of foreign lands and seas, old friends,
old books and things far off
to both eye and mind. Without respite
I could not have pursued for twenty years
such a stubborn course, prey as I am
to this weak noddle and such uncertain health.

How it pains me to observe in my children
the effects of the powers of inheritance
that elsewhere in my work fill me with wonder.
When baby Charley died and after the first sharp
pangs of grief, Emma and I could only feel thankful
that his days of suffering were brief;
sickly since birth, in all the eighteen months
of his life he had never learned to speak
one word and could scarcely even crawl.
We know too well what it is like to have
an invalid child: Etty's recovery
from an unnamed fever contracted two years ago
has been so slow I often despair
she will ever be restored to health.
Fully five of my—now it is only seven—children
are plagued by an irregular pulse,
gift of the Darwin side of the family.
Well I am afraid that the variety *Homo sapiens
darwinii* may soon join the ranks
of extinct creatures and I will not wonder why.

But my children, oh, I could go on long about them,
singing their praises, how exact and wise
they are. You remember years ago
how my older sons discovered the discrepancies
in my micrometers, those traitor tools,
and saved me from dreadful blunders.
Now Etty, that jewel of a girl, like her mother
a genius for language, helps me penetrate
the mysteries of German grammar.—
Those wretched Germans deliberately complicate
their speech. This fact has been confirmed for me
by Dr Hildebrand who writes his mother tongue
as clearly as if it were French.—
Frank, too, has been aiding me lately;
I am so clumsy and his small deft hand
is much better suited for the scissors.
He has been cutting up for me Professor Roger's

beautiful map of North American geology
and together we weighed the pieces
of the continent. I have devised this simple method
to arrive at a proportion of metamorphic rock and granite
for my discussion of the gaps in the geologic record.
How much easier my task would be
if all the links connecting species to species
were buried somewhere deep within the layers of the earth
to be uncovered one day and prove my theory
absolutely—but is science ever like that?

I have complained—and egotized enough
about my own dear ones—I should be glad
to hear sometime about your boy whom you love so—
much love, much trial, but what an utter desert
is life without love.
                    Adios,
my dear Hooker, do be good and wise,
and be careful of your stomach, within which,
as I know full well, lie
intellect, conscience, temper and affection—
                                    C. Darwin

SEXUAL SELECTION

Today I entered the great sub-kingdom of the Vertebrata;
all day I have studied fish, dissected them, read about them
in books and journals, in letters from my expert correspondents
who patiently answered all my detailed questions, compared
male and female fish, wondering always what causes the differences
between the sexes. I am mad with delight having a whole new class
of creatures to consider. At luncheon I could hardly eat my soup
for thinking of the feathery gills, pectoral fins, the hooked
jaw of the male common salmon. Now at night, I lie in bed awake
while Emma sleeps the good, well-earned sleep of the wife
and mother; she snores softly, and pictures of fish as accurate
as Mrs Cameron's photographs appear in my mind as if I dreamed
awake. Mr Warington's loving estimation of the male stickle-
back—he says it is beautiful beyond description—returns
to me and Emma swims by, a gigantic pale fish, her scales shiny
and wet, the quick flick of her fins as she swims off, smiling
slightly at my enthusiasms. And I imagine myself a male fish.
I dart around her in every direction, and then back to the nest
I have made for her. I return to her again; she continues her
strong, steady, idle swimming, amused by my ardour. I push her
with my snout, pull her by the tail and side-spine, I am mad
with delight, I will do anything. I am bright green and blue,
belly and throat carmine, my scales are lustrous like metal,
and I feel my skin translucent, thin, my fishy body slippery,
aglow with an internal incandescence as if my love resided
hot in my simple heart, in my muscles, all my organs, in my tail
and fins, even in my bones, not merely in my mind—
the thoughtless love for the female of my kind.

THE DESCENT OF MAN: DOGS, APES AND ANTS

> *It may be freely admitted that no animal is*
> *self-conscious, if by this it is implied that*
> *he reflects on such points as whence he comes*
> *or whither he will go, what is life and death,*
> *and so forth. But how can we feel sure that an*
> *old dog with an excellent memory and some power*
> *of imagination as shown by his dreams, never*
> *reflects on his past pleasures or pains in the*
> *chase? And this would be a form of self-*
> *consciousness.*

The tender chickens, grown so big, so grand, think themselves
cocks and hens. Jemmie, even, with his delicate sensitive capable
hands, so brilliant with machines; Bessy, my stay-at-home, my
downy bird; they have all revolted, laying their diabolical plan.
Just when Mammy and I were most happy to have our restless, wandering
progeny returned to the nest, they called us into my study; William and Body
like Devil's Chaplains, seated at my desk, informed us that they
were too ancient, too dignified to call us by our birth-right names,
Mama and Papa, that henceforth and forever more we were to be known as
"Mother" and "Father." I would as soon be called "Dog."
Shocked, I slunk away like a cur with what remains of my tail between my legs.

But today I have reclaimed my green table to recommence my essay on man.
At this moment I am disinclined to raise our traitor species much above
its wormy, fishy beginnings, to sing praises of our so-called exalted brain.
The man, who rejects with scorn the belief that his canines' shape is due
to our early forefathers having been provided with these formidable weapons,
will probably reveal by sneering the line of his own descent. For though
he no longer intends to use his teeth in battle, he will unconsciously retract
his 'snarling muscles' to expose them, ready for action, prepared to fight
    like a dog.

Confound them all! My head begins to sing violently.
As the turnkey remarked, "Life is a rum thing."
Ice packs on my spine bring no relief. I have little faith

in doctors—my father was the only one whose advice I trusted—
hardly three or four days pass without my thinking of him—
but his death at eighty-four did not cause insufferable grief
since I had known years in advance that his death was slowly drawing nearer
and nearer—but the death of child—that is a sudden and dreadful wrench—
how I wish I could have been left alone for five minutes
in our old greenhouse last summer for I know then
I should have seen him in his wheelchair as if he was seated before me—
his shrunken bulk—red evening sun behind him.

Now where are my old notes on mind? —
With respect to free will, seeing a puppy play,
cannot doubt that they have free will, if so
all animals, even an oyster has. Now free will of oyster
one can fancy direct effect of organization, the capacity
it has to sense pain and pleasure.
If so, free will is to mind what chance is to matter.
Dog whines, so does man; dog laughs for joy, so does
dog bark; when opening mouth in romp, he smiles.
Thought, etc., implies existence of something in addition to matter
because our knowledge of matter quite insufficient
to account for the phenomena of thought.
We see particle move one to another and that is all we know
of attraction—we cannot see an atom think!
Instinct is memory transmitted without consciousness—
permanent secretion of thought. —This memory, especially general kind
taking pleasure in virtue because acquired in past ages,
seems to indicate that when we turn into angels
imperfect memory becomes perfect, we look back to definite action
in our conscious selves. Such memory may go back to animals
which changed into man—they meet their reward!
Shepherd dog has pleasure following its instincts, pain if held.
If tempted not to follow, by greater temptation, if *memory
of its own emotions* (which intimately must be connected with
reason) would feel subsequent sorrow, whatever the cause had been.
I say grant reason to any animal with social and
sexual instincts; with passions, must have conscience.
Dog's conscience not same as man's conscience

since original instincts different. Man has
some instincts—revenge, anger—which experience shows
for happiness he must check. With lesser intellect
were preservative—no doubt necessary—but now like other
structures slowly vanishing. Our descent then origin of
evil passions. Devil in form of Baboon our grandfather!
Faults of fathers visited upon sons! Society a hive of bees!
—Pain and disease in world yet we talk of perfection!
—Why does emotion cause tears to fall?
—Do female monkeys care for men!
—Does Mr Wynne believe in dogs?

It grieves—it terrifies me to disagree with Wallace so.
But this is too strange. Without his name on the *Quarterly* review
I should have thought his remarks were written by someone else.
It gives me a cold shudder to recall I almost sent him these
and he actually sent his notes to me. But this is not such a jolt
as his fateful letter, received twenty-two years ago: "My dear
Mr Darwin....I hope this is as new to you as it is to me....
if you think well of my essay please send it to Lyell."
And I feared I had lost all priority. We could have been rivals,
but Wallace is nobly free of all feelings of envy or jealousy
(mankind's greatest failing)—he is too modest and now gives me
all credit for Natural Selection. It is remarkable,
especially when I think if he had had my leisure
he might have done as well or better. It haunts me still
that when I omitted, through simple inadvertence, his name
from the first edition of *The Origin of Species*, he did not even chide me.
Now he murders, though not entirely, his and my own child:
"In the brain of the lowest savage, and as far as we know,
of the prehistoric races, we have an organ little inferior
to that of the highest types. But the mental requirements of savages,
such as Australians and Andaman Islanders, are scarcely higher
than those of many animals. How then was an organ developed
so far beyond the needs of its possessor? Natural Selection could only
have endowed the savage with a brain but slightly superior to that of an ape,
whereas the one he actually possesses is but little inferior
to that of the average member of our learned societies."

No, Wallace no! —This from the man I would apply to
in any difficulty about caterpillars, butterflies and birds.
His brain is a stew of brilliant reasoning and trash!
I fear we will never quite understand each other—
but I don't want to offend him—so say:
Man in the rudest state in which he now exists
is the most dominant animal that has ever appeared on earth.
He has spread more widely than any other highly organized form
and all have yielded before him. He manifestly owes this superiority
to his intellectual faculties, to his corporeal structure,
and to his social habits. Through his powers of intellect
articulate language has evolved, and to this his wonderful advancement
is mainly due. He has invented various weapons, traps and tools,
to protect himself and obtain his food. He has made rafts and canoes.
He has discovered the art of making fire. These several inventions
by which man has become pre-eminent are the direct results
of the development of his powers of observation, memory,
curiosity, imagination, and reason. I cannot, therefore, understand
how Mr Wallace can maintain that Natural Selection
could only have endowed the savage with a brain
little better than that of an ape.

I confess I was not totally unprepared for this "heresy."
That paper four years ago in the *Anthropological Review*
cast light on the drift of his mind: "From those infinitely remote ages,
when the first rudiments of life appeared on earth, every plant
and animal has been subject to one great law of physical change.
At length, however, there came into existence a being
in whom that subtle force we call *mind* became of greater importance
than mere bodily form; a being, in some degree superior
to nature, who could keep himself in harmony with her,
not by a change in body, but by an advance in mind.
Man is, indeed, a being apart. We can anticipate the time
when this planet will produce only cultivated plants and domestic
animals, when man's selection will supplant natural selection,
and when the ocean will be the only realm where that power is exerted
which for countless eons has ruled supreme over all the earth."

How can Wallace draw an imaginary line and place man
on one side—dogs, apes and ants on the other?
Of course Lyell, who gave serious reflection to my sneering question
whether he believed the shape of my nose was designed,
hails Wallace's suggestion that a "Supreme Intelligence"
(something like man but cleverer) has guided the stream of variation
to produce our intellectual and moral nature. My mind
can no more digest such statements than my stomach can lead.
This spiritual business clouds his reason. The dead are dead.
We Darwins have long stood fast (thanks to our stone-cold feet)
but now, alas, Hensleigh joins Wallace in seance after seance, testing
scientifically, they believe, its validity. Three cheers
for the wise Allens—Aunt Fanny says that mediums are jugglers.
Spirits, she concludes, do not meddle with matter.
When furniture and heavy bodies move, it is matter that moves them.
I must treat Wallace's views fairly—but it is hard—
he strays from the domain of science. Should I say:
No scientist can measure spiritual powers, rather
I shall endeavour to show that the mental faculties
of man and the lower animals do not differ in kind,
although greatly in degree. But this does not justify
our placing man in his own kingdom, which I will illustrate
by comparing the mental powers of two insects,
a coccus and an ant, which certainly belong to the same class.
The female scale insect whilst young attaches itself by its proboscis
to a plant, never moves again, sucks the sap, is fertilized
and lays its eggs. That is its whole history. In contrast,
it would require a large volume to describe the life of an ant.
But briefly I will specify a few points: ants communicate with each other,
several unite for the same work and even to play games. They recognize
their nest-mates after months of absence, feel sympathy for their comrades.
They build great edifices, keep them clean, close the doors at evening,
guard their domain. They make roads, tunnels under rivers
and temporary bridges over them by clinging together.
They collect food for the entire colony, and when an object is too large
for the door, they make the door larger and later repair the breach.
They go to battle in regular bands, and sacrifice themselves freely

for the common good. They emigrate according to preconcerted plans.
They capture slaves. They move their eggs and their cocoons
into the warmest parts of the nest to hatch them quickly,
and endless similar facts can be given. All these diversified instincts,
mental powers and affections arise from an extremely small mass
of nervous matter, for the ants' cerebral ganglia are not so big as
one quarter the size of a pin's head. From this point of view,
the brain of an ant is one of the most marvelous atoms of matter
in the world, perhaps more so than that of a man.

I could go on long about ants—but back to the business at hand.
Won't Wallace be savage about my moral sense, which, of course,
is derived from social instincts, for who is unconscious of the opinion of
    others;
think how readily we criticize our fellows, how we dread blame but love
    praises.
This instinct like all others was acquired gradually through Natural
    Selection,
at what period I can only guess—but ponder the power of the phrase, "Good
    dog!"

How humiliating is the slow progress of man—I don't know why but
it would give me infinite satisfaction to believe mankind
will attain such a pitch that we should look back at ourselves
as Barbarians—then comes Thomson like a ghost, robbing me
of the time my theory requires. Four hundred million years is not enough
for all the slight changes needed to produce the higher species.
Fear of my own death pales when I think of the sun cooling
and we all freezing. My pet horror: to imagine
the progress of millions of years, with every continent
aswarm with life, with good and enlightened men, all ending in this—
with no fresh start until our planetary system is converted again to red
    hot gas.

How will my book end? Wallace says the organ of man's mind
was prepared in advance. An angel must have come down
and told him that. Gentle—say only—
The world, it has often been remarked, appears as if it had

long been preparing for the advent of man: and this, in one sense,
is strictly true, for he owes his birth to a long line of progenitors.
If any link in this chain had never existed, we would not be
what we are today. Unless we choose not to, we may,
with present knowledge, approximately see our parentage.
And we need not be ashamed of it. The simplest organism
is much higher than inorganic dust under our feet,
and no one with an unbiased mind can study any living
thing, however humble, without being struck with enthusiasm
at its marvelous structure and properties.

There is but one kingdom—there is no kingdom—

Haven't I worked enough?
Where's Emma? Isn't it time for lunch?

REGRETS AND PLEASURES

I have been looking over some of Elizabeth's very old letters
and it is not a cheerful occupation—one gets one's head
too full of times past which always entails regrets,
and now I feel we daughters made a mistake in not talking
to our father more, in not trying more to get inside his head.
I reread the letters our aunts wrote at the time of his death—
it was July then too—and I find it is not the date but the
weather, the look of the sky, that makes an anniversary for me.
Aunt Fanny—then as now, there was no barrier between her heart
and her heart's expression—she wrote: "I feel it almost as necessary
as breathing to express my deep tenderness to you at this awful time.
Poor Bessy! I feel for her that she cannot grieve for him
as she would have done in time past—to my mind your mother's
life is sadder than death." And Aunt Jessie (dead now too)
was always so wise in her feelings: "Why sorrow should make us shy
is inexplicable to me. Is it that strong emotion of any kind
keeps oneself perpetually in one's own mind,
so that one cannot help but feel as if one were equally
in the mind of others: on stage as it were?"
It is the sound of my father's voice that comes back to me,
even and low, the bass tones rich like clay.
It was that sound as much as the feel of his dry,
warm, large hand that assured me there was no trouble or
grief he could not handle. But we thought him rather awful:
his upright manner, his judgment clear and certain,
his reserve so thick sometimes it was as if he was encased
in silence. I can't help myself; half in wonder I repeat
to my children Sydney Smith's curious saying: "Wedgwood is
an excellent fellow—it's a pity he hates his friends."
And I know my mother was anxious lest she vex him.
But that was not right—there never was a more indulged wife....
It is sad at present to think of Elizabeth, her eyesight
failing so badly there is nothing she can do but sit.
Small wonder she seems so troubled—but why
she says she would like to have everything past wiped out
I cannot fathom for her youth was exceptionally smooth

and busy and happy. Despite any sadness in the past
I would not forget. Such a morbid state of mind
I'm sure she would have escaped if not for this slide
into blindness. What a blessing the veranda has proved.
We are cool here under the glass roof, shaded
by the lime trees. As summer keeps blazing away,
the grass is burnt brown but the flowers bloom
like stalwart children proud in their gaudy,
fine new dresses. I know what I will do—
I'll send my piano over to her house and teach her a few
simple tunes by heart so she can play
without needing to read music. I cannot bear to see
her idle, with nothing useful to occupy her hands or
mind—not Elizabeth who has always been the backbone
of the family, despite her twisted spine—not Elizabeth
who never let infirmity keep her from the pleasures of life
or from its duties. But who would not be susceptible to
happiness with the sun so hot, the air full
of a heady perfume. The bees hum greedily
as they suck the lime flowers, feeding and feeding
until they fall to the ground, drunk on nectar.
They lie in a blissful stupour like men after Sunday dinner
but are a danger still to heedless children who roll over
each other like dogs in grass. I wonder why the black caps here
sing a different tune than they do at Maer?
Who would not be cheerful hearing the sounds of summer,
the rattle of the fly-wheel as the bucket is raised
in the well drawing water for the garden, the rhythmic thwack
of the ball and racquet (the breeze rustling the leaves
is like the hiss of fire), Charles' breath
deep, regular and slow as he naps with Polly,
her insistent, indignant terrier bark
stilled for the moment so I may think and sew.
How it amused me to see among those letters from long ago
one I sent, describing to Elizabeth the first dinner I gave
as the young scientist's wife: "Mr Lyell is enough
to flatten a party, as he never speaks
above a whisper. So everyone is obliged to lower

their tone to his. Mr Brown, whom Humboldt calls
the Glory of Britain, looks so shy as if he longed
to shrink into himself and disappear entirely.
Not withstanding those two dead weights, that is,
the greatest geologist and the greatest botanist in Europe,
we did very well and had no pauses." In the thirty odd years
that have passed I think it would not be too egotistical to say
I have acquired more patience with men's foibles. This too
is the weather of Fanny's death: the sky like a scrim, blue
and far away, but palpable nonetheless, a thin
light cloth holding heat to the earth, the portulacas
happy in this atmosphere, their jewel-like flowers
on the end of red stems, opening and closing
as the sunlight waxes and wanes, their leaves
spiky and swollen. The loyal phlox blooming generously
no matter how little care they are given.
It is the world so alive that I associate with
Fanny's death—my almost twin sister,
until I was twenty-four and she twenty-six,
she was my companion in nearly every pleasure.
Our *Mrs Pedigree,* I reread her old lists—
of temperatures (this summer is not nearly so hot
as in '23), words in foreign languages (*surabondance,
ravioli*), her lists of daily chores and household
memoranda (in that we could not have been more
different—Mama called me *Little Miss Slipslop*).
I recall writing at the time of her death that
any memory of her was sweet and unmixed with bitterness,
and I took some comfort from the fact
that she had been gentle and happy but her spirits
were weak, and she would not have borne up so well as the
    rest of us
under the sorrows of a long life on earth—and that
this separation made the next world seem
a reality to me. Oh, when one is young some things appear
so simple. Did I imagine one slipped from this
life into another as if one entered a room already warmed
by fire? I wonder what Heaven is like?

Does Fanny think about me still or is she too content
to long for someone she once loved on earth? I do regret
that my faith has dimmed in all these years.
I should not be so naive as to think we will meet
in bodily form—but how odd it would be
to be reunited once more with my Fanny, she a girl,
a *Doveley* still, and me an old woman, probably
deaf and bent, grown careless of my dress,
my hair a mess—I wish I could be sure,
not plagued by doubts about my duties in this world
and my place in the next. I wish I was truly wise
like Aunt Jessie. She wrote Elizabeth:
"The kingdom of Heaven is no place—but a state,
the peace of God in one's own heart. Expiation
is a necessity to me and not to God. There are those
who have never willfully sinned, therefore
they cannot feel this want. Christ has said
He was not sent to the whole, but to the sick.
So then, it is not true He considers us all
sinners. I find in the Bible all my heart desires
without believing every word of it is inspired."
But I puzzle over the problem of whether
it is better to keep or not keep Sunday,
whether I may, with an easy conscience, play patience
or knit. On the side of doing as I think right
and not considering the opinion of others
I can list the sincerity of showing myself
as I really am, the real good it would do
not to have artificial sins, and my belief
that England would benefit morally
for having some amusements on Sunday. It is a relief
that since *The Descent* has gone into a second printing
and sales of *The Emotions* are brisk,
Charles has been much improved in health
so that these Sundays are truly gay and restful.
I no longer hesitate to invite guests, and next week
we expect dear Body and Litch and their walking party
from the Working Men's College for tea and singing.

Charles' experiments on the power of movement in plants
do him a world of good. Now he is absorbed in *Desmodium gyrans,*
that funny twitching plant, and last night before retiring
we visited the greenhouse to see it asleep.
It was dead asleep except its little ears which played
the most lively games, such as Charles had never seen
in daylight. Most experiments, I confess, I find
tiresome—the careful measuring, the counting—but these
are much more interesting to me and I know how it pleases Charles
to exalt plants in the scale of living creatures.
I wished we agreed more on the place
of man in nature. We must have strawberries
but can I find enough for fifty? In these last books
it amused me to see our children and our pets
transformed into a work of science.
What proud father ever studied so closely
his babies' every grimace or troubled to describe precisely
each contorted muscle in their face as they lay bawling?
It does seem odd that anyone belonging to me
should be making such a noise in the world.
Already Leo plans his trip with the Royal Engineers
to observe the Transit of Venus—he is eager but I feel
rather flat, one is so awfully used to New Zealand.
Oh, occasionally I do believe myself remiss as a mother,
I have so little ambition for my sons. My fondest hope
is for them to be happily married. The roses
are just over and I miss their scent no longer mixed
with the smell of hay and lime blossoms the way
one misses a dear friend after a satisfying
visit—you can almost hear their voice
in your head.

TREE OF LIFE

I was not unprepared for his death;
ever since the attacks he suffered last winter
it had seemed possible—our secure happiness
was shattered. But as spring came that fear
passed away, I believed he would recover
his strength, keep working, more letters, more books.
"I am like a gambler, I love a wild experiment."
Even earlier, we had had our warning.
Last summer during our holiday on Ullswater
he climbed a rock to watch the boaters
and a fit of dazzling came over him. At home
he had me write Mr Wallace: "It was charming,
but I cannot walk, everything tires me, seeing scenery,
even reading much. What shall I do with the years
left? I have everything to make me happy
and content, but life itself is wearisome."
I thought it a temporary depression.
For then he took to studying roots, to training
earthworms, which amused him, although he made
no progress since they neither see nor hear. This reminds me
of all the queer things he tried: how, to answer a reviewer
who doubted that a baboon who adopted a cat, after
the cat scratched her, examined her naughty child's paws
and proceeded to bite off the offending weapons, he
tried it himself and found he could seize with his own teeth
the small claws of a five-week-old kitten.
Or when studying the cause of tears, he asked our boys
first to scream loudly, then contract their face muscles tightly
to see if they could make themselves cry. Or the time
he had Frank play his bassoon for the sensitive plant
to test its seed-leaves' reaction to vibrations—
I often wondered, is this science?
The sudden end was a blessing: the last few days
had gleams of cheerfulness we neither could have felt
if we were entirely aware of his condition.
I am wading through Emerson as I really wanted to know

what transcendentalism means, and I think it is that
intuition is before reason, or facts.
It certainly does not suit me, as Wedgwoods
have no intuitions. And as I grow older
more and more I understand only what
is before me, what I have touched, what I can see.
John Lewis was here all week building cabinets.
I asked to see him, wanting to apologize that the coffin he built
was not needed. Poor Mr Lewis was uncomfortable
thinking it pained me to speak of his death. But
since I persisted at last he blurted out,
"I made it just the way he wanted, all rough,
just as it left the bench, no polish, no nuthin'.
The other you could see to shave in."
I would have preferred him buried in that half-hewn coffin,
buried here at Downe, with a rough stone,
rough block of granite only to mark the spot.
But the rest of the world it seemed wanted him
honoured more in death, buried in a great church,
surrounded by great men. I don't regret
I didn't attend the funeral. That was no place for my grief.
It is here, in this house we reshaped, in the trees—the mulberry,
ash, the beech—the lilacs we planted and saw grow tall,
the apple orchard—our early Kentish Beauties. In the walks
we took, the now vanished hand that reached out, pulled me up
the flower strewn bank, the paths we knew so well in each season.
The poets are wrong. Dying is not like autumn:
leaves turning brilliant, then dropping, drying.
Death is not like winter: the frozen ground, blanketing snow.
It is not sleep. It is the terrible unmoving,
terrible calm, terrible silence of the body—
that was once a person you knew. Even in the final suffering
you knew them. "I am not in the least afraid to die,"
his dry whisper. "I am so sorry for you but I cannot help you.
Tell my children to remember how good they have all been to me."
And he told me again everything I had been to him—
nothing I can repeat although Frank has urged me
to write it down. Now it is autumn.

The weather is magnificent, dry, the sky
violet-blue. The sharp air seems to enter the bone.
The elm leaves glow. Dust motes rise in a shaft of sun.
He once wrote during such an autumn, "I am tired of
fine weather. I long for the sight of mud."

How I hate Thackeray's women. He makes them behave
in a detestable manner which he thinks quite right.
I rejoiced when that tiresome Helen died and there was an end
to all the praises and raptures. "Poor Mother,"
said Etty, "now you have time enough." I try
to make stages in the day, fixed things to do
at fixed times: Bernard's lessons, reading with Bessy,
a short walk out of doors—but I miss
my daily occupation. It comes with a wave of desolate feeling
that there is nothing I need do. Bessy, bless her, does not try
to distract me—she knows me well enough. She told me the funeral anthem
was composed expressly for him, words taken from Proverbs: *Happy*
is the man that findeth wisdom and the man
that getteth understanding. She is more precious
than rubies: all things thou canst desire are not
to be compared to her. Her ways are the ways
of pleasantness and peace. She is a tree of life
to them that lay hold of her: and happy is everyone
that retaineth her. Keep sound wisdom
and discretion: when thou liest down
thou shalt not be afraid. Yea,
thou shalt lie down and thy sleep
shall be sweet. Nor did Bessy hesitate
to recount how William, chief mourner,
seated in the first pew—in front of the nation—
feeling a draught in the Abbey, placed his
black gloves on his balding head.
I do like to picture William that way.
"Girls and boys come out to play...."

The fatal attack came at midnight. He had me fetch
his amyl nitrate from his study. When I returned

he was not conscious but brandy revived him.
Frank brought the surgeon who stayed until morning.
I took an opium pill and rested.
Etty and Frank stayed by his bedside offering sips of whiskey.
He kept dozing off. At half past three Etty called me
when he fainted. I revived him with three teaspoons of whiskey.
He struggled to sit, I tried to get him to lie down,
but when he wouldn't I propped him up with pillows.
His eyes closed, his breathing grew thicker, louder,
more desperate. Downstairs the doorbell rang.
The doctors had returned but could do nothing.
Then the breathing stopped.
I heard my own quiet breathing, wind in an old ruin,
the clock ticking. Watched while the doctors finished
their last useless business. Replied to their awkward
words of sympathy. Embraced Frank and Etty,
then went to tell Bessy it was over.
And calm her violent despair. I did not cry then,
I felt empty of all but that quiet air
coming and going, that small movement of lungs.
No blood in me, no thought, no feeling.
It was not until William and George, and Leo and Horace
arrived on Thursday, not my boys but full grown men
weeping, that something let go inside me
and I could cry. *And the Spirit and the bride*
say, Come. And let him that heareth say,
Come. And him that is athirst come.
And whosoever will, let him take freely
the water of life. In their deep grief I could see
they could not spare me and my life
was valuable again.

III. EPILOGUE

DAUGHTER'S TRIBUTE

I received her last letter: "Sick on Sunday;
well again today, Monday." On Thursday night
she wound her watch as usual, placed it on the bedside table,
laid her head back on the pillow, closed her eyes,
and never woke again in this world. Bessy, of course,
was with her, was the last to see her alive, help her
unpin her hair, wish her good night. The next morning, it was
her body and not her body that lay in her bed. When I arrived,
it was my mother and not my mother I saw, dressed
and laid out, the hands motionless on the chest.
Frank, George, Horace, Bessy, all there before me.
My mother was all things good. Bessy is, of course,
completely distraught; she cries all day long
and can do nothing. Her hands are constantly aflutter—
like a pair of squabbling sparrows. I am angry.
What does God think He is doing?
I have arranged everything, found a minister with common sense,
settled my mother's affairs. I cleaned out her desk,
decided what to destroy, what to save. All the letters she kept,
her diaries, everything that may contain her spirit
I will take. Bessy can have her shawls, her caps, the furniture.
My mother was all things good. In her youth
she was gay and carefree, not above a practical joke.
But I remember her as grave, beset by the anxieties
of our many childhood illnesses and my father's poor health.
Reserved: to strangers she appeared stern, aloof.
I have no clear recollection of her playing with us—
the jokes, the merriment all came from my father.
But now a picture comes to my mind of the parlour furniture
pushed to one side, the rug rolled up, and a troop of
little children galloping to a tune of her own composing.
She never minded childish messes. And she sang to us,
nursery songs—"When Good King Arthur ruled the land...."
"There was an old woman as I've heard tell....
and if she's not dead she's living there still."
Courageous, rash even, in what she let us do.

William was taught to ride without stirrups and thereby suffered
several bad falls. George, at ten, was allowed to go
the twenty miles from Down to Hartfield alone.
And I, too, wandered the woods and lanes by myself
which at that time was not quite safe for a little girl.
My mother was all things good. Calm, serene:
she understood that life's uncertainties
did allow for hope. Always comforting,
she never offered false comfort, false praise.
Fair, honest, blunt: an enthusiastic guest once thrilled
how she must enjoy watching Father conduct his experiments—
"No, I don't." My mother was all things good.
She was definite in her religion, in all her opinions.
Shakespeare, Milton: tiresome.
Tennyson: less so. Coleridge: revolting—
a mixture of gush, mawkish egotism and humbug.
So I had to learn poetry from my husband.
Although poets are, I fear, a lazy lot,
not as accurate as they should be, or perhaps, a bit stupid.
I have not found one poem that could not be improved.
Her sense of duty was strong: she had a large clientele
in the village. But I doubt whether she was any real help
since she never inquired closely about them
and many were people of bad character.
She didn't care much for art or higher education.
(She never tried to get the best teachers for us.)
What she cared for was comfort and Nature and affection.
She made the most of little pleasures: her delight
at the first taste of spring. I do remember clearly
that summer afternoon she called me to the window
to watch two blue titmice leapfrog over each other on the lawn.
I will hunt the stinkhorn in her honour. And, of course,
she thought it abominable to be brutal to animals.
Mounting a crusade to abolish steel traps used in game preservation,
she offered a prize for the design of a humane trap, but no new
da Vinci, no James Watt came to light and the reward went unclaimed.
My mother was all things good. She would do anything
for her servants and their relations. Each summer

she invited the cook's blind daughter to spend
a month with us and they discussed life in the Asylum.
My mother was all things good. She was
splendid in grief: when my father died, to us
who knew how she lived in his life, how
she shared each moment as it passed, she seemed
wonderfully calm, perfectly natural. Only in letters afterwards
could she find words to express her sorrow. And even she was amazed
she could enjoy life still—the good summer weather,
flowers in bloom, the clear bright colours of their petals.
She suffered her desolation alone, not wanting to be thought of
or considered, but to be left to rebuild a life as best she could.
And rebuild it she did, setting up a winter home in Cambridge,
making new friends. And now that the burden of love
she had taken on gladly when young was lifted somewhat
her sense of mischief returned. "I attended the downfall
of the great elm over the Lodge, and a grand sight it was,
especially when it took matters into its own hands and crushed
a good-sized sycamore instead of going the way they were pulling."
Or when she told me how the explanation she gave Bernard
of the play *Electra* shocked Price the butler.
"Is it nice?" Bernard asked. "Oh, yes, very," she replied.
"What is it about?" "A woman who
murders her mother." No—I understand nothing.
My mother was all things good. She was the one who taught me
our God is a benevolent God. Then what about this suffering?
He made darkness pavilions around Him, dark waters,
and thick clouds of the sky. I understand nothing.
But what I cannot swallow is: I had no chance to say good-bye.

PARTIAL LIST OF SOURCES

WORKS BY CHARLES DARWIN:

The Red Notebook of Charles Darwin. Edited with an introduction and notes by Sandra Herbert. Cornell University Press, 1980.
Metaphysics, Materialism and the Evolution of Mind: Early Writings of Charles Darwin. Transcribed and annotated by Paul H. Barrett, with commentary by Howard E. Gruber. University of Chicago Press, 1974.
The Voyage of the Beagle. Edited by Leonard Engel. Doubleday & Co., 1962.
The Origin of Species. Introduction by Julian Huxley. New American Library, 1958.
The Descent of Man and Selection in Relation to Sex. The Modern Library.
The Expression of the Emotions in Man and Animals. Introduction by Konrad Lorenz. University of Chicago Press, 1965.
The Autobiography of Charles Darwin. Edited with appendix and notes by Nora Barlow. W.W. Norton & Co.,1969.
The Life and Letters of Charles Darwin. Edited by Francis Darwin. J. Murray, various editions.
More Letters of Charles Darwin. Edited by Francis Darwin and A.C. Seward. J. Murray, 1903.

WORKS BY OTHERS:

Peter Brent. *Charles Darwin: "A Man of Enlarged Curiosity."* W.W. Norton & Co., 1981.
Ralph Colp Jr. *To Be an Invalid.* University of Chicago Press, 1977.
Emma Darwin: A Century of Family Letters, 1792 - 1896. Edited with commentary by Henrietta Litchfield. J. Murray, 1915.
Sandra Herbert. "The Place of Man in the Development of Darwin's Theory of Transmutation." Part I, Vol. 7, 1974. Part II, Vol. 10, 1977. *Journal of the History of Biology.*
Peter Morton. *The Vital Science: Biology and the Literary Imagination.* George Allen & Unwin, 1984.
Gwen Raverat. *Period Piece.* University of Michigan Press, 1991.
Alfred Russel Wallace. *Natural Selection and Tropical Nature: Essays on Descriptive and Theoretical Biology.* McMillan & Co., 1895.
───── *Man's Place in the Universe: A Study of the Results of Scientific Research in Relation to the Unity or Plurality of Worlds.* Chapman & Hall, Ltd., 1904.
───── *My Life.* Dodd, Mead & Co., 1905.
───── *The World of Life: A Manifestation of Creative Power, Directive Mind and Ultimate Purpose.* Chapman & Hall, Ltd., 1911.
───── *An Exposition of the Theory of Natural Selection with some of its Applications.* McMillan & Co., 1912.
Earl Morse Wilbur. *A History of Unitarianism in Transylvania, England and America.* Harvard University Press, 1952.
Irvine Williams. *Apes, Angels, and Victorians.* McGraw-Hill, 1955.